THE SALES REVOLUTION

Ingrid Maynard

'Anyone looking to enhance long-term revenue growth should read *The Sales Revolution*. Ingrid provides valuable insights into sales challenges and presents a transformative approach involving the entire company for significant growth.

'I highly recommend this book to all leaders aiming to align business functions effectively to achieve lasting results.'

Shaneel Deo, Managing Director, Milliken Australia Pty Ltd

'*The Sales Revolution* is a "must-read" for leaders in all types of organisations. It's written in plain English, and Ingrid lays out a process to make a real difference in our business community. This is written for board members, CEOs, sales leaders, and many more. Everyone needs to join the Revolution!'

Jerry Kleeman, CEO and Director of Kleeman International, Leadership coach and mentor

'What Ingrid doesn't know about sales isn't worth knowing!'

Bob H. Nordlinger, Chair, Superior Strategy Pty Ltd

'I loved reading *The Sales Revolution*. An intelligent, applicable, and essential concept for organisations of all sizes. Sales teams simply must have support from functions across the entire company to deliver engaging outcomes that magnetise and retain their customers. Ingrid's dedication to the role of sales and its importance has been her leading purpose and passion throughout her career. *The Sales Revolution* encapsulates her significant experience and holistic view of how sales must be embraced by all in business, to create organisations and relationships that matter most to others.

'This book is true thought leadership, that once read, must be acted on if you want your organisation to matter in the years ahead.'

Jenny Stilwell, Strategy adviser, business mentor, and author of The 7% Club *and* Small Business CEO

ABOUT INGRID MAYNARD

Ingrid Maynard is out to change the status quo and the future of sales. She knows the time is ripe for a revolution towards customers, sales and profit by transforming how the next generation of market leaders embraces key stakeholders.

Ingrid has an impressive 25-year track record of transforming business outcomes in record timeframes for some of Australia's and New Zealand's most iconic brands. As founder and managing director of The Sales Doctor, Ingrid works closely with sales teams, sales leaders and business leaders: these are her people. And she respects them very much because she understands that in these roles, you never get to pass go, and you're only as good as your last deal or quarter. It's what inspires her to do the work she does, being selective about the companies she works alongside.

Featured on Sky Business, Ticker News, a regular contributor to *CEO World*, the *Daily Telegraph* and *Herald Sun*, Ingrid's thought leadership and commentary on business impacts and the future of work are widely sought after.

Ingrid lives on the Mornington Peninsula with her beloved husband Jason, her musician son Charlie and their cat Leo and turtle. She loves running, walking in nature and lying for hours on the beach reading a good novel.

This is her first book.

Dedicated to my husband, Jase, and my son, Charlie,
who don't really even know what I do ☺ and have
allowed me to 'get in the writing zone'.

Thank you to Claire, Bianca, Renee, Stacey and Chris for
helping to grow The Sales Doctor and The Sales Revolution.

But most of all, this book was written for Dave.
You know who you are ☺.

Disclaimer
The material in this publication is of the nature of general comment only, and does not represent professional advice. It is not intended to provide specific guidance for particular circumstances and it should not be relied on as the basis for any decision to take action or not take action on any matter which it covers. Readers should obtain professional advice where appropriate, before making any such decision. To the maximum extent permitted by law, the author and publisher disclaim all responsibility and liability to any person, arising directly or indirectly from any person taking or not taking action based on the information in this publication.

CONTENTS

IT'S TIME FOR A NEW APPROACH TO SALES

I love businesspeople.

I love those of us who create something out of nothing and make it successful, through working smarter, working harder and achieving what we didn't even know we could. I love the people who join companies with a heart that seeks to contribute – to give. Their goal is to add, to make things better than before they were there.

I love leaders like you who wake up some days and ask, 'Do I really have to go to work today?' and then show up for their companies, teams and colleagues anyway. I love that on other days you are reminded why you're in leadership when you see your impact, your team's impact and their growth, knowing you had something to do with that.

You're my tribe.

I love salespeople most of all. I love them because it is one of those roles in which you never pass go: you're only as good as your last deal, month, quarter, year – your last *whatever*. Your results are everyone's business, and without you there wouldn't be a business. I love that you are the face of the brand, and I love those of you who are so damn good at what you do, it makes buying from you an actual pleasure.

We're now facing a time we've never faced before. While we've certainly seen hard economic times and while we're not necessarily in an official 'recession' – just a per capita one – it's tough going in business right now. For the first time in a long time, companies are letting people go. They're 'restructuring' as they look for efficiencies. Decisions have more scrutiny because there's more at stake now. Costs of doing business have gone through the roof, and people are in that category too. Getting something wrong can mean there is no coming back from it. That's where we are.

Now, as much as I love salespeople, they're not equipped (for the most part) for the conflation of factors businesses currently face, and neither are the companies they sell to or work for. We have five generations in the workplace selling and buying and running companies.[1] Go up or down more than one generation and it can be like talking to someone with a totally different paradigm. The truth is, that paradigm difference is probably very real. And conditions are tougher. There's a weariness everywhere. People are looking for shortcuts when the long way around is actually the most direct path.

As you'll read throughout this book, it's no longer enough for sales to be the only people in the company aware of the impact they have or actively working on their positive impact on customers. That's simply not good enough anymore. Unless we change the way everyone shows up at work with a customer consciousness and with real commercial competence, we will end up in a commercial graveyard of businesses that woulda, coulda and most definitely shoulda.

It's why I created The Sales Revolution. It's a company-wide approach to ensuring everyone is commercial in the way they deliver value to those they serve. It goes deeper and wider than simply being customer-centric, or having a service mindset. Those topics make consulting firms rich and speakers booked

---

1   See chapter 6 for more on this.

but do little to help companies do things differently from the top down.

And they must. *You* must. You *can*.

I've written this book as a 'how-to' guide to help you understand, get those who matter on board, implement The Sales Revolution methodology, and overcome the inevitable scepticism and pushback you'll encounter because it will require work. And I'll show you how to make it stick and what's in store once you do.

I've broken it down into five parts that you can work through to digest how we got here (because unless we understand that, we won't understand the need to change and change fast), what The Sales Revolution is and isn't, how to make the case to your business to go on this journey, things you must avoid doing that are tempting to do because we all love silver bullets, and how to embed the magnetic culture of customer you'll have created.

All along the way, there are stories and insights from top business leaders, sales leaders and salespeople, as well as those who come at my philosophy from different perspectives to bring this to life for you. My goal is to have a conversation with you. To unpack the 'how-to's' across each leg of this journey so by the end of the book, The Sales Revolution seems so obvious you'll wonder why it took me to put pen to paper to bring it to life for you.

Above all, my goal is to make you glad I did, because if you implement the lessons in this book, your company, your customers and your people will have a passion for your business like they didn't and couldn't before.

Let's go, folks.

PART I

WHY WE NEED A SALES REVOLUTION

Revolution is a strong word, isn't it? I could have said we need an Evolution, but I didn't. Because a revolution by its very definition means a complete transformation of the status quo. That is what I'm proposing. I strongly believe that the conflation of economic, social, psychological and – dare I say it – spiritual influences we're experiencing in the world right now mean that treating only one of these aspects would be of little value. A paradigm shift in the way we think about our roles, how we approach our roles and how we deliver the results of those roles to the people we interact with matters so much more than it ever has.

The world has shifted. Those of us who lived through Covid and the lockdowns imposed on us knew that we emerged on the other side different somehow. Some of that difference is better and some worse. Businesses, households, families and workplaces everywhere changed forever.

For us to know that on one hand, and then to return to tinkering around the edges of old methodologies or even to not see the interconnectedness of everything we are and do is wilful ignorance, and in business, spells oblivion.

So, I use the word Revolution deliberately indeed. It is a totally different way of operating as a business towards all those we serve: internally and externally. The Sales Revolution forces us to think more broadly about the way we do what we do, so that we operate from the perspective of value delivery. And not just in a 'fluffy' way, but in a *measurable* way.

When everyone can see the measurable value they deliver and, in turn, receive from those who serve them, it changes the way we show up and the way we're able to appreciate others.

True cost is understood and clarified. So is true benefit.

By focusing on that measurable value delivery, every person in every business knows their contribution to the total, and so is better able to focus on those elements that contribute to that value and expedite profitability.

It literally revolutionises a business's results, culture and people.

Will you join me?

CHAPTER 1

'SALES' HAS BECOME A DIRTY WORD

The scenario I'm about to share is all too common. I invite you to see if you recognise your company, your people or even yourself in any of the following.

'THAT'S NOT MY JOB. I'M NOT IN SALES.'

The only reason this customer was still trading with my client was because they trusted their account manager. Let's call him Wally. The customer had even said as much in emails: 'The only reason we're still working with (my client) is because we trust you, Wally.' Verbatim.

Why was it the only reason?

Because they had been waiting months (about four) for an API to link my client's app to a payment app that is standard for many online retailers, which make up a reasonable amount of my client's customers. Now, waiting is one thing, but when promises for a date when the configuration would be finished keep being extended, it wears a bit thin. Each time an expected date was given to Wally, he'd communicate that to this customer, only to later have to rescind that date, provide a new one – and then do this over and over. And over. Wally was always the one responsible for going back to the customer to tell them the news, and therefore he was the face of each let down.

'It's ruining my personal reputation with them,' Wally said to me in frustration. He's right. It was.

Despite apparently being an expert in this app's integration my client's IT manager did not seem to have any sense of urgency, nor an understanding of the business cost of not getting this done in the timeframe he was setting, and of a constantly changing timeline.

Now that would have been a hard enough barrier to overcome, but as happens so often in sales, these situations sometimes seem to 'pile on' at the exact times we really could use a break. This was one of those.

Because in addition to all of this going on in the background, that customer also recently appointed a new GM who may have something to prove. What makes me say that? Well, not only had he come from working for one of the world's largest organisations to this smaller one, his attitude towards others was on the dismissive and arrogant side.

This little extract will tell you all you need to know.

Well – it did me!

Wally brought this man a coffee on their first meeting and took a punt on how he liked it. The response was: 'I take my coffee black. Note that down for next time.'

So yes, you're right – he was a dick. But he was a dick looking for a reason to put his stamp on everything in the business – including the area Wally managed. That made it very tricky for Wally given the already shaky ground he was on through no fault of his own.

Wally decided he needed to demonstrate that he took this issue seriously by setting up a meeting with their GM, Wally's contact in the business who trusted him, and take a couple of people from the business to explain where they're at with the app integration. His intention was to add some weight, deliver certainty, and set the account back on track.

However, what happened when Wally asked the IT Manager (the integration expert who had already caused a delay of four months) to come to that meeting along with the GM Sales? He was met with: 'That's not my job. It's your job. I'm not in sales. You are. You deal with it.'

It's not like there weren't significant benefits for my client having this integration done either. In particular: it would enable them to make it super easy for new businesses (especially online ones) to come across *and* that integration adds to their stickiness. In the current market, these are big business benefits.

And yet: 'it's not my job' was the response.

I wish this was rare.

Sadly, it is all too common.

It's why I'm writing this book, folks. Because while sales has a lot of work to do in this tight (some might call it a 'down') market, it's not the only factor contributing to the customer experience, to customer retention, to salespeople's belief in what they're selling, to profit, to shorter sales cycles or to improved conversion rates. Any other function that has an impact on the customer must also be aware of that impact and take action accordingly.

IT, finance, production and the like may not see themselves as 'being in sales'. And while they're technically right, it's time for some relearning about their significant impact on sales today and in the future. Because the reality is that the customer is *everyone's* job – either indirectly or directly. We all have customers, and everyone in the company has a responsibility to understand the impact their role plays in contributing to revenue, profit and growth. Unless that happens, companies will fail.

When any other function or a leader points to sales as solely responsible for customer-driven metrics, they may also know deep down – even if they can't pinpoint exactly who or what – that the solution is much deeper than that.

The time has come for a sales revolution.

Will you join me?

WHEN SALES HAD PRESTIGE

One of my favourite mentors is a man named Jim Rohn. He was the first 'thought leader' I'd ever seen live. For those of you who might not know him, he was Tony Robbins's mentor. So yeah, we're going back about 30 years here.

Now, this man made his fortune being a salesperson. He too had a mentor, J Earl Shoaff, who taught him that to grow his income he must learn how to grow himself. The more Jim took on from his mentor and put into his life, the more success he started to have in his career, the more sales opportunities he was able to take advantage of and the bigger his personal wealth became.

I say this because he operated in the days when sales had prestige. It was widely understood and accepted in all organisations that those in sales were important. Without them, sales wouldn't happen – and without sales, the company wouldn't exist and therefore no one would have a job. Salespeople, especially good ones, were respected. They could command large salaries and earned commissions because they backed themselves and their abilities to generate the revenue their companies relied on.

The reality is that without sales, it's pretty hard to have a company, organisation, club, business, not-for-profit ... Every organisation needs sustainable revenue growth. And that revenue doesn't generate itself. Even today with the best AI or online presence, it requires an iterative understanding and appreciation of customer needs to keep customers buying because they value the outcomes they receive. It seems to me that many companies and the people who work within them have forgotten this principle. I think they need reminding. These days it's pretty normal to hear:

- *'I don't want to be too salesy.'*

- *'Do I sound like a car salesperson?'*

- *'Never trust a real estate agent.'*

- *'I'm in business development, account management, client services, partnerships ... '* – rarely sales.

Sales has literally become a dirty word. Is it a career to aspire to? Well, not anymore – it seems it's become a stop gap until something better comes along, or something people 'fall' into. There aren't many children these days who will even know that sales is a career, let alone tell their classmates that's what they want to do when they grow up.

To me, this is a terrible shame, even though I understand it. There aren't many positive role models we can even look to who might make us change our minds. And yet, when you stumble across someone who absolutely loves selling (yes, there are still people like us out there), they bring us along on a journey we're delighted to go on and make us feel like few others in business can. Skills and qualities I fear we haven't necessarily lost; we've just forgotten their importance.

I'm out to change that. I say I'm on a mission actually, and for a whole host of reasons. Fundamentally it's because we really need sales and we really need to look after our customers. Frankly, they deserve better. The art of being of service is almost gone. Customers suffer, but so do we who are able to be of service because it's a glorious feeling when we make someone else feel special, even if only for a few minutes.

The world has changed. Business has changed. People have changed.

And while I know change is the only constant, the rapidity of that change today forces us to look at what we're doing and how we're doing it, and ask ourselves some key questions:

- Is how we're approaching customers sustainable given the market, the economy, the last four years, the current sentiment?

- If not, what needs to change?

- Is the definition of customers in need of change?

I love questions. They force our brains to get active looking for answers.

Have a look at your company. Now look at your sales team. Are they up to the challenge we're all facing in the toughest market conditions since the nineties? When you look at each person's performance, do they have the skills to *create* opportunity; I mean *actively unearth* opportunity in a market that will continue to tighten? Are they willing to change their approach? Do they even know that change is required? Are they willing to do the work that comes from doing something differently?

The feedback I receive from most sales managers I speak with every day is that while they have a team that may have the capability, it might lack the mettle to do what will now be required of them.

And that, folks, is a big problem.

You probably already know that, right?

So, where did all the good salespeople go?

WHERE DID ALL THE GOOD SALESPEOPLE GO?

It's a question I've been scratching my head pondering for the longest time. Because it's not a recent problem – it's just that we're really feeling it right now, when we need good salespeople the most!

A little while back I interviewed another of my mentors on my podcast 'The Sales Revolution' about this very issue. Bob Nordlinger is one of those rare birds whose CV makes most of us feel like we're not trying very hard: Bob is the CEO and Consulting Director of Superior Strategy – he's had his consulting firm for around 30 years. He was a 28-year veteran Chair of one of the longest TEC groups in Melbourne – TEC 12. The Executive Connection (TEC) is now known as Vistage International. It's a group for CEOs and business leaders who come together to work on their companies with peers, guided and coached by an experienced leader.

Bob was a guest lecturer at the Centre for Defence and Strategic Studies at the Australian Defence College on and off for four years. He was adjunct professor at the Australian Graduate School of Entrepreneurship at Swinburne University for nine years, specialising in strategic management in MBA and MEI programmes.

It's safe to say strategy flows through his veins! In addition to these accolades he was the visiting professorial fellow at Monash University, again specialising in strategic management, international business operations and systems thinking. Bob is both ex IBM and ex McKinsey Consulting. He has turned around five companies, including John Holland, and was also the CEO of two startups. He hails from the US, but Bob has called Australia home since 1975. I am proud to be a member of his BOB (Beat Other Businesses) group.

He certainly knows a thing or two about business, about strategy, and certainly about sales. Here's an extract from my conversation with him which helps us to understand the slow decline in the status of selling as a profession to aspire to:

You know, when I was growing up, and obviously that was a long time ago with all this grey hair, sales was an honourable profession. You know, my father, after World War Two, when he came out of the Air Force, he was an aeronautical engineer and he took the national sales management job at a jet engine company, Fairchild Engineering. And jets had only been invented during World War Two. So, it was a new thing. And he was professional. He was proud. The salesmen at the car dealerships that my parents bought their cars from – they were professional. They took initiative.

But you see, once marketing became the driver of sales or perceived as a driver of sales, sales reps were just there to take the order and to learn the techniques to close the deal as quickly as possible, and they were paid accordingly. Suddenly the reason to be in sales was you could get high commission. You could probably earn more money. It attracted people who could earn more money, but it was always on a transactional basis.

Sell this, get paid, sell that, get paid, sell another one, get paid.

And that's how it evolved.

So, it's no surprise that a different sort of person was then attracted into sales and given a different sort of sales training. And that training became all about techniques. And I even know companies where the sales manager's office was called the 'killing room'.

And *if* you needed to get a customer over the line, you'd say, 'Well, look, I think we can do a special deal. Let me take you into my sales manager's office.' And of course, they got the customer in that office and that was considered the killing room to get that customer over the line. Is it any wonder the perception of sales as a profession and salespeople as professionals began to be eroded over time?

This is why we must regroup. **It's time to go back to the drawing board and not just tinker around the edges rejigging old models.** What we need now is a complete transformation in the way our companies think about customers and how we engage with them. If we don't do something radically different, we won't just get left behind – we could become irrelevant to the very people who once paid us money for the services they valued or the products they loved.

I don't want that to be your company.

CHAPTER 2

ORDER TAKERS AND GLORIFIED CUSTOMER SERVICE PEOPLE

The market we're in now I liken to recovering from a flood: the water level has started to subside and now we're confronted with the dross, the silt and so much rubbish. Once hidden under all that water, it now can't be ignored because it's exposed for all to see. It's an eyesore. If we leave it just sitting there it'll stink. We've got to deal with it.

A RISING TIDE ...

When everything is going well, it's easy for leaders – sales leaders included – to look good. Business is smooth; money's coming in relatively easily and budget pressure is low. Hard conversations aren't as common and certain behaviours tend to get a pass because we're profitable. Even bad apples are left alone, especially when they're good at selling. We tolerate them, and leave them to it.

All to our detriment.

How we operate in good times will determine our success in hard times.

What exposes the true capability level in any business is how well it responds to and handles challenge. And this is certainly true when it comes to the capability of a sales team.

I was at my executive group the other week and we were looking at the organisational structure of one of the other members, a CEO of a biomedical research company. Someone asked him: 'If you could choose five people that you could probably let go of, maybe even be glad to let go of, would you know which people you'd choose?'

The answer was an immediate yes. But the CEO had some reluctance. He felt that letting them go would be a betrayal of the 'culture' he felt he'd sold them on. He was also a bit concerned about the potential impact it would have on company culture, on perception beyond these five people. None of that changed the fact that he still could identify five people immediately.

What does that really tell us?

I think it tells us that we 'carry' underperformers until we simply can't. I believe that many businesses are at that point right now.

Consider the following questions in relation to your business:

- Does everyone in your company deserve a place?

- If you had to choose five people to let go immediately, who would you choose?

- If you had to, would you be able to do a rough calculation on everyone's return on capital?

- What about your team?

- What about the sales team?

- Would you be able to just know whether or not each person is delivering more value to the business than they're being paid?

It's uncomfortable, isn't it?

Nevertheless, we must ask ourselves questions like these – and answer them. It's too important. I'm not trying to be dramatic, but there's too much at stake: our company's livelihoods and the livelihoods of all those people who work with us may depend on your ability to do that.

I warned you that I love questions, so here's another couple for you:

- If asked, how likely is it that each person could articulate the measure of value they deliver to your business?

- Do they treat the business itself like a customer who matters to them?

WHAT IF OUR EMPLOYEES ADOPTED A FRACTIONAL SUPPLIER MINDSET?

Fractional service providers are starting to pop up everywhere on LinkedIn.[2] The time is ripe for companies to re-examine how they use human capital: who *really* needs to be a full-time employee? Which roles can we outsource to a fractional supplier?

Using an agency that charges less than a salary to deliver more value is a compelling proposition, especially when the board is putting pressure on the CEO to deliver profit and sales.

Not bragging, but I actually predicted the advent of a fractional workforce but I called it 'the rise of the ABN workforce' a little over a year ago, in light of the need to respond to the talent shortage companies everywhere were facing. It's essentially the same concept. Besides solving the talent shortage, I also like this approach because fractional suppliers also mean:

- the company becomes a customer, which changes the dynamic and the expectation of both parties

---

2   A fractional service provider is a professional who offers specialised expertise on a part-time or contract basis, allowing businesses to access high-level skills without the need for a full-time hire. These roles are commonly used for positions like CFOs, CMOs and CTOs.

- the fractional supplier is evaluated on their performance in a different way to an employee

- the fractional supplier knows it's only as good as its last gig and needs to keep performing to keep having a gig

- it works for both parties, and when it doesn't, it's easier to part ways and move on than it is with an underperforming employee.

So, what if our employees adopted a fractional supplier mindset? Better still, what if they *behaved* like one? What if they had to continually demonstrate to the company (their customer) measured value delivered?[3]

If most economists are right, we're going to be in this tight market for about two years. If mining companies are shedding staff[4], if big IT companies are too[5], it's a sign to the rest of us that soon we will all know someone who has lost their job or is at least worried about losing their job.

It needn't be this way.

I propose something else.

I propose The Sales Revolution as the antidote to so much that we face now and will continue to face. What if instead of what we have right now, every person in our company:

- knows who our customer is and what their role is in delivering value to them (either directly or indirectly)

- knows who their direct customers are (internal or external) and how to uncover what matters to them

---

3   If there are any union leaders or members reading this, maybe I've put myself on your hit list! Please know that I'm not trying to decimate the years of negotiating you've done with companies to get the amazing conditions Australian workers enjoy. I'm not. What I will say is this relationship, like any, must adjust and change with the conditions and situation.

4   https://www.abc.net.au/news/2024-07-17/andrew-forrest-fmg-fortescue-announces-700-job-cuts/104110506

5   https://www.npr.org/2024/01/28/1227326215/nearly-25-000-tech-workers-laid-off-in-the-firstweeks-of-2024-whats-going-on

- is able not to just simply deliver value to those customers, but unpack with them a measure of the value that has been delivered to them so it's real for both?

If you're paying attention, you'll already see that this goes beyond sales.

It's why The Sales Revolution isn't merely a zuped up version of customer centricity.

It is deep.

It is wide.

It is a way of being.

Companies that undertake The Sales Revolution become magnetic: they attract the right people and repel the wrong people (for them). They bond with those who want to belong because there is an alignment of purpose. These companies are steeped in what I call a 'Culture of Customer™' and have a 'Customer Consciousness™'. These are the companies that are unashamedly themselves and, as such, become impossible to replicate and difficult to catch.

HOW DID WE GET HERE?

I'm getting ahead of myself! That happens when I'm excited!

Let's come back to traditional sales for a moment, and what I mean by order takers and glorified customer service reps. They're everywhere in sales teams today, regardless of industry, age or experience level.

How did we get here?

Bob summed it up in my conversation with him, but in the nineties, marketing became the flavour of the month, year, decade, quarter of a century ... in fact (and this makes me look like the yokel I clearly was in year 12), I wanted to 'do marketing' at university even though *I had no idea what it was!* It's embarrassing to say that, but it's an example of how much marketing became the thing to do and the answer to all business challenges. As Bob would say, 'Marketing was the glamour job'.

And I did 'do marketing'. While I got the marks to qualify for the degree, I 'wagged' most of my first year and failed my Commercial Law assignment so badly that to pass I needed a high distinction on the exam! By the time the exam rolled around I'd already decided marketing wasn't for me (they weren't my people, I'd decided), but if I wanted to transfer to another degree I had to pass. Guess what? I did pass. Shame on me for being so damn lazy! But I might also have been writing this book about marketing instead ☺.

Anyhoo.

The business thinking back then was that marketing would educate our customers, and if it was working, would create demand for our products and services. That meant that all sales really had to do then was 'take the order' and 'keep the customer happy'.

And so started the steady erosion of skill, technique mastery, and strategic thinking. And here we are today.

Many of you may be able to relate?! (Come on, I know you do!)

Order takers are okay when times are good and money is flowing in. Order takers tend to be nice enough people who get along well with our customers, who may even have a good personal relationship with key decision makers and stakeholders. They may ask questions on good days and do a lot of 'telling' on bad days ... Unfortunately, more often than not they possess only a shallow ability to dig out opportunity and create a reason for customers to buy from them. Order takers tend to avoid pushing back or challenging customers because they fear upsetting them. They equate a good working relationship with niceness, lowest price or discounts and product availability.

Today's buyers are pressured. On a daily basis they're juggling multiple high-priority issues. Their available budget has shrunk because the cost of doing business has skyrocketed, with increasing wages, higher interest rates, higher utility prices and higher rents. Covid lockdowns eroded their war chests.

This combination generates greater scrutiny over all buying decisions.

Getting 'it' wrong means more now. No one wants to make a mistake. If a decision turns out to be the wrong one, that budgeted money can't be redirected because it's gone.

Even if buyers get 'it' right, just **how right** has that decision been? Are they able to demonstrate a measured return on that investment? And is that return aligned with the company's number one or number two goals, or is it nice but irrelevant – rendering it not valuable?

So I'd argue that even if we were just investigating salespeople in this book, there is a bunch of work to be done there to get the ones we have up to muster to be successful now. For the most part (and yes, I know there are always exceptions), the skillset on average is shallow. Since lockdowns and remote working became a 'thing' I've witnessed a lack of salespeople who are willing to stretch themselves. Something must change. And *fast*.

The answer isn't to simply get rid of these people because, frankly, who will replace them? Salespeople with deep and wide skillsets and experience are looking to retire soon because they're at the other end of their careers. They're not looking to 'ramp up' activity levels and go hard. That's what they did 30 years ago in the recession we had to have.

So if you want a better sales team, you will need to arm the ones you have now with the qualities and skills to go to war with more than a stick. You will need to grow your own. The benefits will be evident down the track. *If* you invest in the *right* people who want to grow, it will be worth it.

More about that later.

What about the account managers? If I asked most of them (and I do) what their role is, they tell me something like: 'keeping customers happy so they stay'. And if I don't lose the will to live at that point, I may ask them how they do that. I brace for impact as they tell me something like: 'well, I visit them every month and ask how everything is, and what can we do better'. And that's why I call them glorified customer service reps. Expensive ones too!

There aren't many Account Managers who say their role is to 'protect and fortify my portfolio' or 'grow my A customers by 10% by focusing on XYZ' or 'increase share of wallet by 5% with 30% of my portfolio'. It happens every now and then, but it's rare.

While there are a tonne of reasons why, here are a few of the most common I've encountered:

- No one has taught them how to approach their portfolios in a way that categorises customers according to **growth potential** (most is on historical sales performance).

- No one has taught them how to uncover those accounts that they are **at risk of losing** (even if it has nothing to do with them), let alone what to do about it.

- No one has taught them how to **fortify and protect** the accounts in their portfolio (beyond being 'nice').

In most cases, it really isn't their fault, because we also have sales managers who have learnt *their* roles by trial and error. They've risen up the ranks as the best salespeople who are then earmarked for promotion to sales manager, *which usually means the company gains an average manager and loses a star sales performer.* And because they simply 'found a way' to be good at what they do, they don't necessarily understand what made them good and therefore how to help others to be good too.

When they don't know what they're doing as managers, they often drop down into their team's accounts and start doing the selling for their team members to improve outcomes. It's what I call 'directing traffic'. Any 'saving' a company makes by not investing in their salespeople's or sales leader's development proves to be **very** expensive. The value of the lost time per person spent waiting for a new sales hire to be productive (and the opportunity cost of internal people's time training them), lost revenue as you watch them struggle, trial-and-error mistakes that cost accounts or account growth or account retention (and therefore revenue and profit), the inability to trust a pipeline which impacts forecasting ... Massive impacts on revenue and margin, and yet companies still argue that it's cheaper to not 'invest' in salespeople or sales leaders. After all, they might leave. But what if they stay?!

From my vantage point, I've just about seen it all.

Good times seem to exacerbate these issues because of the 'everything is fine' phenomenon. There is no pain ... yet. Even though the revenue could be two to three times more, they're satisfied with it coming in with little hassle when there is enough 'fat' to deliver easy margins because cost pressures haven't been like they are now.

It's all good ... until it's not. And it's not good right now.

I wish my business had its greatest demand when the economy is strong – but we don't. Companies don't want to 'look under the bonnet' when times are good.

In a down market however (like the one we have right now and will have for a while), every dollar and every hour counts. Who can afford to lose customers or people? Revenue and productivity must be maximised, and costs minimised. It's the reason my solutions become essential in times like we're in right now – they work. They're based in reality and get businesses better faster.

Let me ask you this: how many of your salespeople understand the concept of cost of sales? Or their contribution to minimising it? What about the concept of customer acquisition cost? Or cost to serve?

Even if they know what these terms mean, do they understand how to operate in a way that improves those profitability levers?

I think they need to know.

Especially now. It's never been more important.

CHAPTER 3

A SCARCITY OF SALES TALENT

Sometimes I wish I also had a search agency for great salespeople, because at least twice a week I'm asked if I know of any good salespeople for roles or good sales leaders. Sometimes it's me putting great salespeople and sales leaders in front of search agencies and prospective companies because I think: 'You have to meet this person.'

It's a reflection of what we've seen coming (those in my space have certainly) because as the kudos went out of selling, so too did the legends of sales. There are a few outliers here and there, but they really are rare birds. The combined impact of a lack of professional development and fewer people seeking out selling as a career choice has left us in a sales talent desert.

WHY *EVERYBODY* IN YOUR BUSINESS NEEDS TO UNDERSTAND SALES

Once upon a time, selling skills were included in induction programs and were as essential as other topics like occupational health and safety, product knowledge, the history of the company, and culture. I worked for The Body Shop Australia in the nineties when it was in its heyday. I loved it so much I would have worked there for free! My leader had to tell me to go home every day, and even questioned my time management skills. It wasn't that at all for me: it was just that I loved it so much it was hard to go home! Such was the cultural fit for me.

As part of my time starting in the training department at The Body Shop, I delivered some of the induction workshops for new staff ranging from guys out in the warehouse and delivery, to store casuals, to new accountants and IT people. Regardless of department, role or seniority, everyone went through the same induction program. And looking back I think the reason was so that every person understood that customers in stores and how we treat those customers (with basic connection skills and steps to selling) was important. It also meant that anyone in the support centre could be counted on to provide additional support at Christmas time armed with some basics. Common business sense.

It maximises resources. It instils the culture from day one, and it reminds everyone why we're here: customers and how we treat them.

While that is a retail example, I'm presenting to you The Sales Revolution Induction Framework™ where the following tenets are explored:

1   Who is our company's customer: who do we serve?

2   Who is your customer?

3   How do we treat customers here?

4   What is value? (How to uncover value.)

5   What is our purpose?

6   What are our products and services?

7   How do we sell those products and services at a high level?

8   How does my role contribute to the company's growth and profit?

THE SALES REVOLUTION INDUCTION FRAMEWORK™

Induction topic	Purpose	Demonstrable skillset
Welcome to the organisation	Founder story/Evolution story	Able to tell another person the story of the business in terms of: • key events in the timeline • why it was started • what has been key to its success and what that looks like today.
	Expectations of our people How to succeed here	Able to articulate how to: • ask for support • work with team members • prepare for and contribute to meetings (internal and external) • how to achieve KPIs and work closely with direct manager • what 'good' looks like by end of first 30/60/90 days.
Our service/product	Everyone understands core product/service and value it delivers to company, customers and all stakeholders How we deliver our customer experience	Knows features and benefits of products Knows how we sell our product/service Be able to present to the group benefits our product/service brings to customers and stakeholders Articulate the role they play in their role to deliver best experience for our customers

Induction topic	Purpose	Demonstrable skillset
What is a customer?	Know our approach to a Culture of Customer™:	Identify all of their customers: internal and external
	• everyone has a customer and is a customer • showing up to be of service • getting to a measure of value delivered • reporting on value delivered.	Micro behaviours of service mentality for their role: • be able to uncover what matters to each of those customers in terms of the value equation: $V = B - C$ • articulate measurable value across the 3 types of value for their role with a key customer: financial, functional, emotional • get to a measure of value delivered for that customer.
Speaking about our value	Be able to speak about the value our products and services bring our key customers with confidence regardless of role	Use our USP structure to confidently communicate the solutions we have for the problems our customers want to have solved
Community	Understand our community is our customer Experience firsthand the value we bring our community	Able to describe the connection between the value the company delivers to the community and how the community delivers value back to the company

If you're reading this and thinking, 'How on earth or why on earth would I or could I possibly get Amy in IT to know these things? Is she ever going to use them in her role? It's not like she's going to go out and sell! Actually I wouldn't want her to sell and she would hate the thought of it! Our products and services are complex: it takes our sales team months to get their heads around them: why on earth would it be covered as a section of an induction program?'

I hear you. But here's the advantage: when Amy is supporting another person in the business, she is more likely to have an appreciation of:

- this person is *my* customer

- I know how to get to the root cause of the issue to solve it properly (so I minimise costs to the business and maximise the benefits)

- I understand how my solution to this problem will also affect our 'end customer' at some point

- this is what our salespeople do all the time: they must have great skills – I actually respect them.

It helps take us out of our silos, out of our own self-importance, and right-sizes us back to being useful, of value and – most importantly in my opinion – of service.

The sales talent shortage is twofold:

- There aren't even enough 'warm bodies', meaning we have a supply issue.

- The ones we do have only have superficial sales skills, which won't be enough in a down market.

There are many reasons for the lack of sales talent. Stay with me here people because we must look at our own backyards for the cause of some of this, and of course for the answers.

When I spoke to 'Steve', he told me something that I've heard echoed a half a dozen times in other companies. What he said was that while his team was hitting targets, he was losing sales talent because when they feedback to the business insights about customers and the market and presented feedback about other areas in the value chain that were 'lacking', it was falling on deaf ears. Nothing was being addressed, which meant that nothing was changing for the customers when experiencing 'service' from other divisions of the business.

These salespeople were no longer willing to put their personal reputations on the line when they knew the company continued to let their customers down with seemingly no appetite to change. This erosion of belief happened over years, not weeks. Once a salesperson begins to lose belief in the company's ability to deliver what they're working hard to do, it affects sales and the retention of good people.

If you're not in sales or never have been, you may not know that our personal reputation matters to us because it's our greatest asset. Our customers may *like the products and services* that the companies we work for provide, but they *form relationships with us*, and when those relationships extend into months and years, it gets personal too. So, when the company repeatedly fails to fix something that is affecting the customer experience, those customers tell the salesperson because that's who they *trust to take action*.

When that salesperson then takes this issue back to the company, and then that issue isn't fixed, they know they've *personally* let that customer down. Nothing is perfect, and we all know these things will happen occasionally. But when it becomes 'a thing', not only does the customer have a disconnect with the company but so does the salesperson. And given enough of these 'let downs', they will leave.

I can just hear some of you saying to yourselves as you're reading: 'Well, maybe it's time those salespeople left', or, 'It's the salesperson's job to manage the customer expectations in those cases'. You know what, it's actually not. **When an issue affects sales but is beyond the ability of the salesperson to change that issue, it's *not* the salesperson's responsibility.** Especially when it's something the company is saying it does or can do and then doesn't.

It's time that the rest of the company cared more about both the salesperson and the customer (and by extension *revenue*). Hello!

It's time to place the responsibility where it actually belongs and then fix it.

You might be thinking: 'Well, what's the big deal about losing a salesperson? I'll just recruit another one!'

Good luck with that project.

When you lose a great salesperson like Steve did, a consistent performer and deliverer of results for eight years, it hurts. Sales leaders know the cost.

Customers start to question why someone so good has gone, which can make it harder to continue to sell to them. Other salespeople lose belief, which makes selling even tougher: belief is a big success factor in selling. I can't sell something I don't believe in because it will come through to the customer. They may not know I don't believe but something won't ring true to them and they'll take longer to buy or won't buy or won't buy as frequently as they would if that concern wasn't there.

Customers talk to other customers or prospective customers.

Suppliers talk.

Employees talk.

I don't know about you, but I've found the theory of six degrees of separation to be more like two in a small country like Australia.

It matters. Whether you think it should or not is irrelevant.

So, what's the upside to listening to the salesperson and customer and actually improving the thing that isn't working? Only an improved or even a great experience, even stronger belief, firmer commitment, better reputation ... up, up, *upside*.

You know that statistic: it is four to seven times more profitable to keep a customer than it is to replace them? How about the cost of having to replace a salesperson – especially an experienced one?

Territories in some cases can remain unmanaged for months and months while you're interviewing potential replacements. This usually means customers in those territories are vulnerable to competitors, which will probably mean losing market share and losing sales. Getting those customers back is expensive and erodes profit.

It takes time for salespeople to know your company, how things work, how things get done, and to know the customers in their portfolios. Even experienced salespeople can take months to be really productive when new to a company (depending on the sales cycle) because it takes time to understand the new stuff – yes, they can sell but that's not all that's required to be excellent.

You may be thinking: 'Isn't it the salesperson's job not to overpromise and underdeliver?'

Of course it is. However, that's not what I'm describing here. I'm talking about the baseline of being able to offer a product or service in good faith knowing it will actually be fit for purpose when it arrives, and receiving and using it will be easy for the customer. I'm talking about communication across the value chain about stock availability or supply. That part isn't about *sales*, but if we want a confident salesforce, our salespeople must know everyone along the value chain will uphold their end of the bargain. In other words, everyone will do their job.

That's not overpromising. That should be the bare minimum standard.

As I said before, we all know stuff happens. Any salesperson will have to manage difficult situations that occur every now and then. It's when letdowns become a constant that they lose belief in the value of what they're selling. They lose trust.

Losing great people always hurts. Nail your great salespeople to the wall, people! Keep them, nurture them, protect them. It is worth it to them and to you.

WHEN IT'S TIME TO SAY GOODBYE

But what about the warm bodies we're carrying who are average at best, or who lack the skill or will to deliver what we need them to?

You can use the following drive/ability matrix to assess each salesperson to determine whether you need to invest in them to 'grow your own' sales talent pool or whether it's time to say goodbye. Those who are willing will find a way and, with your support, will grab the opportunity to be better. Those who aren't willing will find excuses. As Jim Rohn used to say: 'It's too hard to pump up those people each week.'

DRIVE/ABILITY MATRIX

	Low ——— ABILITY ——— High
High (DRIVE)	**What to do:** Provide in-field sales coaching / Invest in sales training **What to do:** Provide: opportunities to stretch / model of excellence / sales mentoring
Low	**What to do:** Have an exit strategy / Begin planning replacements **What to do:** Performance manage / Create opportunities for self-awareness and ownership

If they're not delivering their targets because they're not willing to do the work, or are reluctant to take suggestions to improve on board and then act on them, or you find that the quality of their work is wanting in spite of investment made in them, it's time to let them loose. **You are better off redistributing their portfolios with great people as you look for someone else, or rethinking how you go to market, rather than 'carrying' people you shouldn't.** Remember, salespeople are your first line of brand ambassadors.

TOP 10 QUALITIES OF GREAT SALESPEOPLE

Once you've evaluated your sales team against my Top 10 Qualities of Great Salespeople, you'll be a bit clearer about which people you want to nurture and develop and you must give them a deeper skillset than the one they needed in good economic times.

Top 10 Qualities of Great Salespeople:

1   They're **hungry**: they make themselves available when it suits the customer rather than themselves.

2   They're **willing to do whatever it takes** to get results, not just 'do their best' (as it might be their best is not enough to get what is required).

3   They're able to **bring more sales opportunities** into their pipeline by having more conversations in the right way with the right prospects and customers.

4   They **maximise the opportunities** they have by multiplying stakeholder engagement, extracting more from each lead and always booking a next meeting from a meeting.

5   They **align the way they sell** to the way each customer buys.

6   They're able to **ask the hard questions** they know need to be covered with a customer.

7   They **ask for the sale, recognising that asking directly is crucial to closing the deal and securing the commitment.**

8   They **believe in the value** they bring personally and in the solution or product they're selling.

9   They're so **rehearsed with the essentials** of how they sell, present solutions, handle objections and tricky issues, and close that they can't (or rarely) get it wrong.

10 They **love selling**: they're driven from within and see every conversation as an opportunity to practise or to learn.

CHAPTER 4

THE OPPORTUNITY A TIGHT MARKET BRINGS

We often carry underperforming people in a good market. We shouldn't because it can cost us our best people, who think: 'How come they take the p*** and nothing happens while I'm busting a gut getting great results?' They're right, you know.

But we do.

Because we think we can.

Good economic times take the urgency out of just about everything. They make companies and the people within them flabby and lazy. They just do.

When challenge enters the picture though, as it has now, s*** gets real. Real quick. And suddenly leaders need to re-examine their people, their procedures and results, and make some better decisions. Yesterday.

No longer is it okay to walk past poor performance.

No longer is it okay to walk past lack of activity.

No longer is it okay to walk past presenteeism.

The placement of responsibility in challenging times tends to come back to where it belongs, which I think is a good thing.

HOW WE DO WHAT WE DO

The disciplines we develop in a down market when continued in an up one will turbocharge your success. You'll have a revamped engine, and good economic times will fuel that engine to blast off!

And it starts now.

In a tight market, what will be the standout is how we make others *feel*. If the *way* we deliver our product or service through our core business directly improves the results for those we serve, our results will also improve. And that is way more valuable in a down market than product or price alone.

For those of you who remain sceptical about product and price, I have a question for you: if product and price were equal between two suppliers, and supply timeframes were equal, what would make you choose one over the other?

It's who you like more.

Who you trust more.

And we tend to trust those we like, but we don't always like those we trust. Remember that.

It comes back to *how we do what we do*. How we are of service to those we serve. How we make others feel in the experience of delivering the product or service. When we are intentional about that, we are willing to cultivate those skills and qualities that will deliver that experience and inspired to deliver that experience consistently well.

Simple? Yes, but not necessarily easy. Although it *is* easier than we think it is. How willing are we to make the necessary changes to create a different and better experience for all those we serve?

Change can be hard, but failure is harder. So is regret! Choose your hard. When we tell ourselves it's hard we give ourselves a reason not to take action. Do you want reasons or results?

In a down market, we need results. Don't give yourself excuses why you can't when there are too many ways and reasons why you can. This book will take you on that journey.

A tight market gives you opportunity to make changes you otherwise wouldn't be able to.

Five actions to take

These are my recommendations to any business that wants to get into shape now and ready itself for the marathon we'll face when the market picks back up:

1. Right size your sales team and revenue enablement people (five people exercise).

2. Put everyone through an induction program to establish a customer consciousness.

3. Teach everyone how to uncover what matters to all they serve and how to unpack and measure value delivered.

4. Reinforce these behaviours with truths for each team, routines that support the right behaviours, and structures that reinforce them.

5. Ensure that leaders are models of excellence when it comes to a Culture of Customer™.

CHAPTER 5

WHY IS GOOD SERVICE SO RARE THESE DAYS?

There is a service deficit wherever we go. When I first started working with Officeworks, friends of mine assumed I was working with the stores and they'd say: 'Oh, their service is great. Is that because of the work you're doing with them? Someone greets you at the door as you go in.'

My work at that time was actually with their Business Team (B2B) so I couldn't stake any claim whatsoever. I'm not here to disparage a very loyal and beloved client for having door greeters, but it doesn't say much about our expectations of service as customers if great service = door greeters! After all, it's just someone saying hello. It's a step in the right direction, but it's a reminder that excellent customer service is rare.

WHAT *IS* GOOD CUSTOMER SERVICE?

So, what do I mean by 'service' and 'being of service'?

Imagine going to a restaurant. The maître d' comes up and makes you feel like they're genuinely glad you're there when they greet you. They talk to you as if they like you, they explain the seating situation, get you seated, get you watered and get you ready to have a lovely experience.

Regardless of whether it's a little café or an upmarket restaurant, none of these things cost money, and each little effort means an enjoyable experience that leaves us as customers wanting to come back another time and wanting to tell our friends about it.

When a market is easy to sell in, salespeople get lazy and focus on product and price. But that isn't service. When we focus on product and price alone, we miss the critical differentiator: the experience. How we make people feel as a result of how we deliver value to them.

Why do we choose to brave the cold and pay upwards of $6 at a café when most of us have coffee machines or coffee at home? We can get our favourite drop of Mornington Peninsula wine delivered to the comfort of our homes, so why would we head out to a bar and pay $15 a glass? What makes us go to a juice bar where we'd pay twice as much for a smoothie we can easily blend at home using a smoothie recipe from Instagram?

We buy the feeling we get when we're sipping or chewing. We're buying the interaction and energy exchange with wait staff and other patrons. We're buying the ether we walk into: the background music, the ambience and the décor.

To quote *The Castle*: 'It's the vibe.'

After lockdowns came remote teams and flexible working, with many of our companies removing front reception staff in direct response to Covid. Formerly referred to as 'directors of first impressions', reception roles were for many an excellent starting point in their careers.

Contrast the receptions of a post-Covid world – where human receptionists have been replaced by machines, taking our mug shots and spitting out a sticker with our name and a QR code on it – with those of the past when you'd be greeted by name, made to feel looked after and expected, offered a beverage and a seat as you waited for the person you were meeting with. How's the new first impression of the company?

All in the pursuit of hygiene and cost cutting – mostly the latter now that Covid is largely behind us. Why pay a person when a machine can do it? We've reduced a *role* into a *task*, when it's clearly so much more. This misses the point: the experience is lost.

How are you welcoming your suppliers, prospective and current employees, and prospective and current customers into your company every day? What does the first impression they have with you say about what they can expect thereon in? Is it a warm one that makes them glad to be there, that reminds them of why they love working with you, or an enticing preview of what working together will be like? Or is it sterile, efficient and practical? How much thought have you even given it?

Fundamental to The Sales Revolution is the understanding that we each have a customer. Our responsibility is to deliver measurable value to each customer by first understanding what that is for them and how to do that well, and then to deliver that value to them consistently.

Without that understanding in everyone from the top down, across and through the business, it's too easy to reduce people down to tasks. This is something we must be aware of with AI: is it adding to the value of the experience or removing something? Being of service is a gift to both the giver and the recipient.

Having a service mentality isn't a 'cherry on top' business ingredient. It's critical.

Whenever there is an exchange of value, with one person being of service to another, you have a supplier–customer interaction. Whether you understand that or not depends upon your education in the value of service beyond product and price.

In a down market a value-based approach is your opportunity to strengthen your bench. You can use the tougher market conditions to grow market share by going that little bit – or a lot – beyond your competitors. The degree of difficulty lies in how well you're able to get your people to come on that journey.

YOU MUST TRULY SHOW UP FOR OTHERS

Here's another truth about service.

Being of service gets us outside of ourselves. To truly show up for the other we must park our egos at the door for a time to be there for them.

To be of service. To give first.

Is your company a place your customers want to belong to? What about your people?

The role that being of service plays in fostering that sense of connectedness is powerful and goes well beyond the sales team. To me, being excellent at business means we are also excellent corporate citizens through the way we serve our customers, our people, our business ecosystem and the very communities we operate within.

We do this in simple ways by being the best versions of ourselves.

While it's great to support digging a well in Africa or to donate a percentage of sales to charities and causes, what can we actually do *ourselves* with a bit of effort to make a difference to others?

Tradeware is one of those special companies. It supports a para-athlete in her efforts towards excellence. Through triathlons the managing director got to know this person and saw the struggle she had raising money to support her to be the athlete she knew she could become with the right equipment and to help with flights and accommodation to compete in events. The focus is simple. It's personal. It's genuine and heartfelt.

That's the privilege we have in business because we can change lives when we are intentional with our focus and purpose. Tell me this support doesn't resonate with Tradeware's staff!? Of course it does.

We can be a place of belonging to those who resonate with our values and purpose, and a company people aspire to belong to as workers and as customers, suppliers, referral partners.

Anita Roddick in her book *Business as Unusual* stated: **'I want to work for a company that contributes to and is part of the community. I want something not just to invest in. I want something to believe in.'**

For those of you who don't know, The Body Shop was a success story for about 25 years, with a store opening every day somewhere in the world at one stage in the nineties – a time when many other businesses were struggling. Its founder, Anita Roddick, came from Italian immigrant parents who understood that their little café was a part of the community of Arundel in Surrey and behaved as such to their customers who were also their neighbours, suppliers and friends.

Anita took these qualities on through osmosis and imbued them into The Body Shop through things like paid community service, Trade not Aid (as it was once known), childcare centres for employees' children, subsidised restaurants for staff, and lots of other ancillary services that made everyone within and orbiting the business want to belong to it and feel like they did.

Her purpose was first to be a good business and to do business the way she wanted to do business. Priority number one.

Because of the way she did things, she was also an excellent global business citizen who lifted up many others through doing business a certain way. It wasn't about creating a business so she could do those things: those things were part of her being a good businessperson.

I think it's time for us to remember that our companies can be so much more than just providers of goods and services in exchange for money. Reimagining how your company can deepen its service mentality could be transformational.

Consider we now have five generations in the workplace:

- Baby Boomers (experience, track record, maturity, stories)

- Gen Xers (hard workers, success seekers, leaders)

- Gen Yers (entrepreneurial mindsets, out-of-the-box thinkers)

- Millennials (tech-savvy, purpose-driven, adaptable)

- Gen Zers (to thine own self be true).

It pays to remember that each generation brings its own value; let's not just pander to one generation and miss out on the collective value that *everyone* brings.

Having said that, Gen Z is one of my favourites because they can see through the bulls*#t. They know how the system works. On a bad day they might 'play it', but if we look to their best they are also seeking personal purpose in the companies they work for and in the work itself. They are looking out for what matters to them and utilising work as part of creating a meaningful life for themselves.

As Trudy MacDonald, Managing Director of TalentCode HR, recently said during our conversation on The Sales Revolution Podcast:

> I think the common perception about Gen-Z is that their focus is doing purposeful, meaningful work, and it's all about saving the world, and ESG is really important to them, and it absolutely is. However ... they've entered the workforce when many countries are in a recession. So job security is actually their focus ... They've shifted away from those macro concepts to focusing on job security.

I think this is good news for companies everywhere. If we treat this generation today as the leaders of tomorrow, consider how impactful The Sales Revolution Induction Framework™ could be on engaging this talent. From day one, you would be building on Gen Z's natural proclivity for meaning and purpose, and their desire for job security and in so doing, hold your company in the best stead now and years from now.

There is a reason you're reading this book. I think you're also searching for that something extra. My goal is to show you how to leave a legacy – whether you're leading a sales team, or selling to customers. Whether you own the company or work within it. You and I will now go on The Sales Revolution journey together.

PART II

MAKING THE CASE FOR CHANGE IN YOUR BUSINESS

If you're anything like 'Steve', you'll be nodding away at what's been shared already and you may even be thinking to yourself: 'That's what I've been saying for years!'

You already know things have to change, and by 'things', I mean the way we sell, the way we treat customers and the way we do business. You probably also know this change goes beyond sales and the people you lead in the sales team.

Making the case for change is a toughie. But I'd like to help you do this because we both know that what's at stake is too important. I know you don't want to watch a great company fail or lose great people because you stayed silent or you weren't able to successfully make the case for change compellingly enough.

Change is something most of us avoid, isn't it? We're told it's the only constant but we still leave it until continuing along the same path is too painful. Change brings with it the discomfort of doing things differently, of challenging our perceptions and perspectives and possibly even 'being' different. It can make us a bit itchy and scratchy. Change can trigger in us a fear of letting go of something that previously worked. We may try to bargain with ourselves by saying things like: 'Well, you know there's no guarantee of success with the "new"! The old may not be perfect but I know it pretty well and it delivers some stuff sometimes.'

Unfortunately, safety thinking like this could send your business in the wrong direction faster than you know. Especially now. So, my goal in this part is to arm you with the tools to have the 'case for change' conversations with your business leaders.

If, however, you're not 'Steve' and you are one of the executive team, or you're on the board or you're the owner of the business, I suggest you use this section to help you communicate The Sales Revolution to get those you need in the business on board. After all, it's not much good if you're the only one who believes in it!

While one person screaming at clouds doesn't change anything, change can and often does start with one person. May that person be you.

To quote the late great Dame Anita Roddick yet again: 'Never feel too small or powerless to make a difference.'

Please take note of the following icons, which will indicate which parts of the text relate to one of the 4Rs™ of The Sales Revolution™:

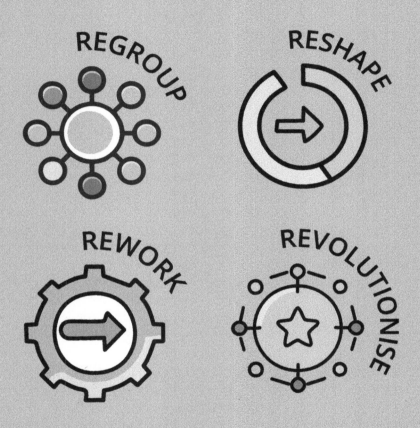

CHAPTER 6

WHAT *IS* THE SALES REVOLUTION?

The Sales Revolution is my response – my solution – to the crisis I believe many businesses currently find themselves in or will soon find themselves in generating revenue, profit and growth. Because we find ourselves in such a totally unique set of circumstances at this point in history, there is no 'playbook' as such. That's why I created my own.

The Sales Revolution is the playbook I'm handing to you.

Is 'crisis' too dramatic? I don't think so.

A COMPLETELY DIFFERENT WAY OF OPERATING

Enterprise-sized companies will be able to weather the storm intact and emerge at the other side of this market okay – minus a few dents and scuffs here and there.

My main concern are the companies that are one or two tiers below. You're the ones that I am speaking to the most. You are the ones who aren't as able to access the sales talent required to grow the revenue you need. And without completely transforming your company into something it currently isn't, I am proposing a way forward.

I make no apologies for frequently referring to The Body Shop in this book. Not because The Sales Revolution is modelled on that business – it isn't. But because I worked for both The Body Shop Australia franchise and Body Shop International in the UK, I know firsthand that the first 20 years of that company came pretty damn close to embodying many of the principles that work.

When I worked for The Body Shop in the mid-nineties, I experienced how the 'magic' permeated every aspect of the business, and most importantly flowed through to the customer experience in store. That was where I came from: the stores. I worked at Frankston where I started as a Christmas casual while studying at university. Upon graduation, I started with the 'People Team' as a Training Administrator covering a maternity leave position. I wanted to be a trainer, having just graduated with a teaching degree. I saw training in the title and I'm not going to lie: I was possibly the most challenged 'administrator' around – but I did get to do the training no one else really wanted to do. I lapped up every opportunity to learn and grow.

Around 8.45 every Monday morning at the office in Mulgrave, we'd all come together around the reception desk near the top of the stairway to have what we called our 'Tribal Gathering'. It was where we heard Barry and Graeme, the owners of the Australian/NZ Franchise, tell us the news of what was happening in Body Shop land in Australia and globally.

Plain talk.

Lots of laughter.

No pontificating.

Each team leader would share their news.

Logoed watches were awarded for five years of service, and we celebrated achievements both business and personal … babies, birthdays, work anniversaries, new hires, new products, campaigns. Judy from the childcare centre below and Louise from the restaurant would also join us and update us on their latest news too. We were all part of that company.

You know what I remember the most though? The way it felt. What made it so special was 'the vibe'. Even now I can go back to that time in my mind in a nanosecond and recall that feeling. I know I wasn't the only one who looked forward to going to work every day and found that the days just flew by. Monday mornings set us up to succeed, and when the Tribal Gathering was done and we returned to our desks around 9.30 most of us had a smile on our faces.

Monday mornings aren't known for being something most people spring out of bed for.

But *I* know they can be.

The Tribal Gathering was also a way to reinforce for everyone in the company that we each had a part to play in its success. To its core it was a customer-focused business where customers were those who came into our stores *as well as* those we served in community projects, our people, one another ...

Of all the companies I have served through my consulting practice, there hasn't been one that does anything remotely similar on a consistent basis. Individual teams might come together to look at *results* but it's not an in-person company-wide thing, and most meetings about numbers aren't all that encouraging or uplifting! I've never seen a company that intentionally celebrates and reinforces its DNA in such a way.

As I look back, I realise that Customer Consciousness™ was everywhere in that business. It was felt and understood by us all.

The Sales Revolution is a company-wide approach to revenue generation, to growth and to profit. It creates a Culture of Customer™ that is holographic in that examining any one person, team, process or approach, all would epitomise this essence – *regardless of function in the company.*

I call it a revolution because it's a completely different way of operating. It's not an event. It's not an evolution. It's a new way of being for *everyone* in the company.

Half measures will avail us nothing. We are at the turning point: we can either stand still and risk the inevitable massive fallout on our customers and people, *or* we can create something different that will elevate everyone and reconnect them with their purpose.

THE SALES REVOLUTION MODEL™

What I'm proposing is not fluffy. It's practical, logical and thoroughly grounded in commercial commonsense and a knowledge of human behaviour. The Sales Revolution Model shows you not only what the methodology is, but the key principles and practices that underpin its success.

THE SALES REVOLUTION MODEL™

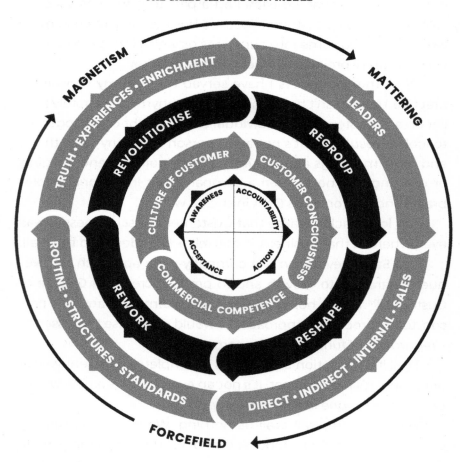

Throughout this book I'll unpack each element of this model so you understand the *why* as well as the *what* and *how*.

The journey to The Sales Revolution reminds me of a story I heard recently about a person on a train carrying a takeaway coffee. As the train took off, the person stumbled and spilled their coffee everywhere: the ground, on other passengers, on the seats, on themselves.

Is the story about the need for us to be more careful about how we hold a takeaway coffee when on public transport? Or is it telling us we shouldn't bring hot drinks onto public transport? Is it to make us reflect on whose responsibility it was that the coffee spilled? Does it even matter?

Well, let's say that the cup represents your company.

The coffee represents what your company is made of.

Had the person on the train been carrying a takeaway tea or a hot chocolate, that's what would have been spilled when they stumbled instead of coffee.

It's what we're made of that spills out when we face the inevitable bumps.

No company will be immune from the bumps that will come in the next couple of years. But I want you to ask yourself now: 'What will spill out when my company is "bumped"?'

The Sales Revolution will fortify your company to its core and reinforce your 'bench strength' throughout. That means that regardless of the inevitable 'bumps', your company will be fine.

Maybe even more than fine.

No two companies are the same though so the way yours transforms through its journey on The Sales Revolution will be unique. It will unify those people who resonate strongly with your company's DNA. They'll be *more* attracted and bonded to it as it becomes *more* of what it is. And of course, external customers will be magnetised in the same way.

You can't half do it.

You're in or you're out.

You will create a Culture of Customer™. That requires shifting *everyone's* thinking and behaviour so that this culture is felt with every customer's experience internally and externally. Major results won't happen on the first day, but they'll be evident way sooner than you might expect because you'll know what to measure – way beyond sales and revenue generation. It's the acceptance and practice by which *everyone* in your company, regardless of role, is a customer who matters, and as such that's exactly how we treat them.

That's why The Sales Revolution is deeper and more far-reaching than 'customer centricity' or merely mapping the customer journey.

Your people will want to deliver more and your customers will feel compelled to contribute because they feel part of it: they belong.

But it's deeper than connection alone.

It's the reason productivity will improve.

It's why growth gets easier.

Same with selling.

And why profit becomes inevitable.

The takers will self-select because they won't resonate with your company DNA. The givers will, though.

You'll be surrounded by people who *choose* to consistently grow to be their best every day.

These people understand that while perspective is subjective, truth isn't. These people take responsibility and accountability for their decisions, actions and impact. These people show up to be of service to others. They love belonging to something that inspires them. They become inspirational too.

Finally, The Sales Revolution brings out the best in everyone; not because it's easy but because it requires *growth*.

The good news is that it's simple and straightforward.

Like any big challenge, we'll tackle it bit by bit.

Are you ready?

CHAPTER 7

BREAKING DOWN THE SALES REVOLUTION MODEL

Let's begin by isolating each aspect of The Sales Revolution Model because there are a few models within the larger one.

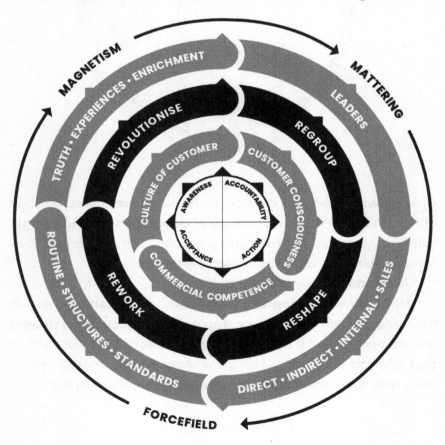

THE GROWTH MODEL™

Consisting of four elements, this has been my coaching recipe for the work I do with The Sales Doctor. Each element feeds into the next.

THE GROWTH MODEL™

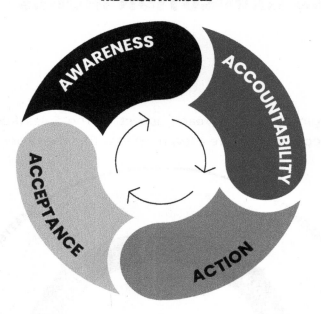

Growth (which requires change) starts with **Awareness.** As good old Dr Phil says: 'You can't change what you don't acknowledge.' Within Awareness are three sub-elements: Self Awareness, Customer Awareness and Situational Awareness.

Awareness is the starting point.

Next comes **Acceptance.** Without **Acceptance** there is resistance, which will delay or stop growth. **Acceptance** doesn't require people to like their new awarenesses or even like the fact that change is necessary to grow. **Acceptance** merely recognises that these new awarenesses are evident. They're true.

Awareness and **Acceptance** set a person, team or company up to grow, but on their own they don't actually change anything. Growth can only happen with **Action,** and two conditions: Consistency and Effectiveness. This is because we don't want our actions to be effective only once. And we don't want to be consistently poor or average with the quality or impact of our actions. We need both.

When human beings take **Action** on our own, we tend to stick to the things that feel good or right (regardless of what *is* right). All human beings have blind spots about our **Actions**. That's why, without an **Accountability** point, the quality and consistency of our actions will diminish. With **Accountability,** we have the opportunity for self-reflection, for discussion, for coaching and for learning. We understand what worked, and why it worked because of the evidence. It allows us to also understand what didn't work and why because of the evidence. As a result, we're better able to iterate because we're linking action with impact.

At this point we'll have come full circle.

Through **Accountability** we have new **Awareness** so the process then recommences at a deeper level.

Each time this process is undertaken, deeper levels of insight and wisdom are attained. New results and new levels of those results are achievable.

Growth is both internal and external.

THE CULTURE OF CUSTOMER MODEL™

The Culture of Customer Model™ underpins The Sales Revolution. Without any one of the three elements, you won't have The Sales Revolution – you'll merely have an improvement in certain pockets of your business and in certain aspects of your business. Permanent change will be difficult.

THE CULTURE OF CUSTOMER MODEL™

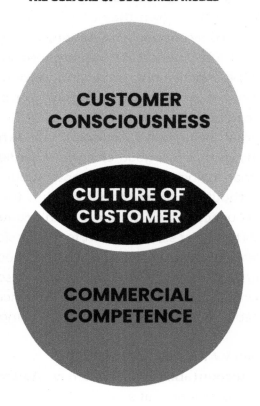

CUSTOMER CONSCIOUSNESS™

Customer Consciousness™ is the beginning.

It starts with the leaders, then those who have direct contact with customers, followed by those who have internal customers before landing on salespeople to ensure everyone in the company understands the three key principles of The Sales Revolution:

- Everyone *is* a customer and *has* a customer.

- Every customer matters.

- Our goal is for customers to matter to us as much as we matter to them.

This stage builds the appreciation that it is logical for the customer to belong to the *company* rather than to one person or even to a team. It clarifies for everyone that having a Customer Consciousness™ is fundamental to individual, team and company growth.

To successfully implement this, everyone in the company must undertake **The Sales Revolution Induction Framework™** that ensures every new supplier and employee is immersed in your **Customer Consciousness™** from day one.

COMMERCIAL COMPETENCE

Commercial Competence is the ability to understand, deliver and unpack a measure of value for all customers. It isn't exclusive to the executive team, to finance, to sales or any one person or function. You must educate everyone about the 10 key metrics of:

1 revenue

2 margin

3 cost of sales

4 customer acquisition cost

5 lifetime customer value

6 cost to serve

7 return on time invested

8 return on capital

9 return on expense

10 return on investment.

When every person becomes clear about their personal impact on each one, it enables them to mindfully, purposefully and deliberately take action that contributes to growth or minimises cost because they understand the impact on *all* customers, including the company itself. Without **Commercial Competence**, The Sales Revolution would remain 'conceptual' and hard to quantify. With it, the culture is infused and enriched with the reality of the **Culture of Customer™**. It keeps it practical, measurable and real.

CULTURE OF CUSTOMER™

A **Culture of Customer™** is the experience customers have with your company, be it personal, process based or with the company itself. They know how they feel as a result: like a customer that matters, because they do. They know they've been thought about before they were even known personally. It's your company's way of being.

Anyone in your company will embody that **Culture of Customer™**.

Any system, process or product will embody that **Culture of Customer™**.

And every time a system or process is used or people in the business's ecosystem interact with your company, the **Culture of Customer™** is reinforced and strengthened.

THE 4RS OF REVOLUTION

The Sales Revolution takes place over four phases (what I call the 4Rs of Revolution™):

1 **Regroup:** Leaders are taken through a series of activities that enable them to assess the gap between current and potential measures of value and assess what that is costing the business now and in the future. Leaders construct, present and implement two quarterly plans of action with their teams to track progress across the seven key metrics and their subsequent impact on the business. In line with **The Growth Model™**, leaders will move through each phase with a particular focus on Accountability: mutual and external. A survey will be conducted at this point across the

business and beyond to measure the felt experience and the tangible value delivered to all customers.

2   **Reshape:** Those with Direct Customers, those with Internal Customers and naturally all those in Sales will be immersed in a workshop series, coaching, tracking and implementation that reshapes their skills, processes and approaches to working with their customers. This phase is a cross between concept and action, which is primarily behaviourally driven to transform ways of being with all customers. When **Regroup** and **Reshape** phases are completed, the company will be immersed in **Mutual Mattering**™.

3   **Rework:** Each team comes together to create its own standards, structures and routines to create a Forcefield that ensures **Mutual Mattering™** is reinforced and continually strengthened across the company. Leaders will share and exchange what they've done to rework their standards, structures and routines with one another to increase the **Mutual Mattering™** with all customers.

4   **Revolutionise:** Closely tied in with a **Culture of Customer™**, this phase works to ensure this culture is consistently experienced by all customers through Truths, Experiences and Enrichment unique to the business. This is when a company becomes **Magnetic**: bonding existing customers and attracting new ones who want to belong because their personal purpose resonates with what the company is radiating. The leaders are trained to facilitate workshops with their teams to create, implement and report on what this looks like for their customers. A survey will be conducted at this point across the business and beyond to measure the felt experience as well as the tangible value delivered to all customers. **A Magnetic company becomes impossible to replicate and even harder to catch.**

CHAPTER 8

WHAT THE SALES REVOLUTION *ISN'T*

Company culture isn't about words on a wall, or having a day where the company comes together to do a series of activities that spits out their values.

Culture is felt. You experience it.

Walking into a culture that is strong should enable anyone to describe what it is. And if you gathered those descriptions, they'd say more or less the same things.

When The Sales Revolution is in full swing, people who deal with anyone in your business will know it has a Culture of Customer™ because it is experienced anywhere and everywhere in the business.

IT'S MORE THAN SALES

The Sales Revolution isn't a process to follow to be better at just selling. It's bigger and broader than yet another model that generates revenue or talks about customer centricity in a way that defines 'customer' only as the one who purchases products and services from us. The Sales Revolution defines a 'customer' as anyone with whom we have an exchange of measurable value when performing our role.

To contrast the difference, I will first of all walk through some very familiar sales models and concepts that have been trotted out over the years.

Let me be clear: I'm not criticising any of the following sales models. What I'm doing is showing that they are *only* sales models, which is completely different to The Sales Revolution methodology. The other fundamental difference is that these models, while familiar, were built in the past for a time that is lost to us forever. They will not be enough to help your business now and certainly not enough for where we're headed.

SPIN SELLING

The key elements of SPIN Selling are:

Situation: Gather information.

Problem: Identify problems the customer experiences.

Implication: Underscore why those problems need to be solved.

Need payoff: Lead them to conclude as such on their own.

SPIN Selling, developed by Neil Rackham, is a powerful sales methodology that revolves around the four stages above. Instead of traditional hard-selling, it encourages salespeople to delve deeper, first gathering essential information about a customer's current situation, then uncovering problems. From there, the focus shifts to exploring the implications of leaving those issues unresolved, before finally guiding the customer to recognise the true value of the solution. By helping buyers reach their own conclusions, SPIN Selling fosters a more engaging, consultative sales experience.

THE MILLER HEIMAN SALES SYSTEM

The key elements of the Miller Heiman Sales System™ follow.

Create opportunities
Conceptual selling
Executive impact
Securing strategic appointments

Manage opportunities
Strategic selling
Strategic selling® government
Negotiate success

Manage relationships
Large account management process
Channel partner management
Diagnosing

People and organisation
Predictive sales performance
Sales excellence assessment

Support and enablement
Sales access manager
Web reinforcement

Management execution
Funnel scorecard
Sales benchmarking
Strategic selling coaching
Conceptual selling coaching
Strategic selling funnel management

The Miller Heiman Sales System™ is a comprehensive framework designed to enhance sales performance by focusing on three core areas: creating opportunities, managing opportunities and managing relationships. It provides structured approaches like Conceptual Selling to align with customer buying processes, Strategic Selling for complex sales, and Large Account Management for maintaining key client partnerships. The system also emphasises the importance of people and organisation, support and enablement, and management execution.

CUSTOMER CENTRICITY

Here is a common model for customer centricity:

- Feedback drives continuous improvement.

- Empower the frontline.

- Designing the experience.

- Metrics that matter.

- Understanding your customers.

- Customer focused leadership.

Customer centricity is all about putting the customer at the heart of everything a business does. It means really understanding what your customers want and designing experiences that meet their needs. This includes giving frontline staff the power to make decisions, using customer feedback to keep improving, and focusing on the important metrics that show how well you're doing. It's also about having leaders who make sure the whole team is working towards keeping customers happy and loyal, creating a business that's always looking to make the customer experience better.

THE SALES ENABLEMENT FRAMEWORK

The key elements of a modern sales enablement framework are:

- customer-centric focus

- building buyer confidence

- multithreaded buying

- digital era adaptation

- revenue support

- talent development

- driving hypergrowth.

A modern sales enablement framework is all about updating traditional sales approaches to fit the digital age and better support buyers. Instead of just helping sales teams close deals, it focuses on guiding them to support customers through their purchase decisions. The key is building customer confidence, because buyers who feel sure about their choices are much more likely to make high-quality, low-regret purchases. This approach helps drive growth by making it easier for teams to sell, buyers to buy, and by developing the skills of salespeople.

The Sales Revolution is a *paradigm shift* in the way a company operates in relation to its customers, both internal and external. As I outlined in part I, how we're selling to our customers isn't enough anymore. My prediction is that most companies will realise that for too long, they've neglected their salespeople and will suddenly want to invest in deeper skillsets for them to cope with a 'down', or at the very least, a 'tight' market.

Losing new sales is one thing, but when a company starts to also lose existing customers, panic can set in. If by the time you're reading this it hasn't, you'll begin to see that panic all around very soon. It's inevitable.

These companies may still ignore the call for a paradigm shift however, and instead turn to some of the models I've outlined above. You now know they won't be enough, and why.

THE BUCK STILL STOPS WITH SALES

Don't get me wrong: when it comes to sales performance, the buck still stops with sales. What we must do differently though is raise awareness from your leaders down and across your company that sales can't do what it does *without other parts of the business supporting it and sales supporting the other parts of the business.*

None of us is an island. We need each other. And that means we need a new appreciation about what role everyone plays in fostering new business and keeping the customers we already have in these new market conditions.

Fundamental to The Sales Revolution is an awareness and an appreciation that everyone *has a customer and is a customer.*

In any business there will be those people who have internal customers and those who have external customers. Those with internal 'customers' can also be known as internal service providers, which includes roles and functions like IT, HR, learning and development, payroll, finance, legal and operations. These roles provide support that enables others in the business to do what they do more easily because they're specialists in a particular area.

Those with external 'customers' include roles such as presales, lead generation, business development, sales and account managers, customer service, recruitment, accounts, marketing, logistics, procurement and elements of operations. Every role supports another role in some way, which is why there is more to uncovering improvement in any 'customer' experience than just looking at one person or one role or even one function.

CUSTOMERS, CUSTOMERS, CUSTOMERS

It all comes back to 'customers'. Everyone must understand that if sales has a problem and it's coming from the customer, it is *everyone's* responsibility in some way, shape or form. The problem must be fixed by the person or function that can. And if it *can* be fixed it *must* be fixed. Future revenue relies on it being fixed. And prospects and customers are the source of future revenue.

You get it.

I know you do.

But when was the last time these truths were discussed and understood viscerally by the leaders of each value function in your business? When a business gets to the point where it starts to hum along, it is easy to develop amnesia and forget the underlying truth of everything: **it all starts and ends with the customer. They are our reason for existing and the source of our sustenance.**

That's why I'm not proposing a change to the process of selling or trying to redefine revenue-generation roles or responsibilities. The change we need extends beyond those whose responsibility it is to deliver sales targets. When we as a company, not just as individuals, treat our customers like they matter to us because they do we get Mutual Mattering™ and Mutual Enrichment™, which are key elements to The Sales Revolution methodology.

Our customers, the community and our suppliers act as extensions of our salesforce when they know they belong and that they Matter. They bring us more customers who are also aligned with our values. They bring us great people to work with us. The line blurs between 'customer' and company. We belong to each other.

Mutual Mattering™ exists when both parties matter equally to one another. Both want to work together, both want to contribute to the relationship, and both are willing to exchange mutual value. What is more powerful is when the company matters to the customer as much as the customer matters to the company. This is when The Sales Revolution has turned the company into one that delivers a congruent experience for the customer at every opportunity and at every contact point.

If this just happened on an individual level, it would be a start.

It would be a fantastic start – but hardly a Sales Revolution!

What *is* revolutionary is when the relationship the customer has with us goes from one with an individual in the company to one with the entire company. With the whole business and brand, but not just the brand. It must be an energy exchange through experience.

It means less risk for the company if their people move on, because the customer's relationship is with the whole company across every interaction over any one individual. **Those relationships are conducted individually but no one individual is holding up the sky.**

Everyone is.

And the sum of the whole is greater than the sum of the parts.

CHAPTER 9

THE RISK OF BUSINESS AS USUAL VS THE UPSIDE OF THE SALES REVOLUTION

Leaders need a compelling reason to change. They need to have the case for change simply and clearly laid out to see two things:

- a continuation of the current state of play will be worse

- what's in it for them and what could be achieved should they make the necessary changes.

MAKING THE SALES REVOLUTION TANGIBLE

One of the ways to make The Sales Revolution tangible is to take one measure of value and illustrate its impact on more than just the sales team and their customers. Making it clear to leaders that even one thing has far-reaching ripples goes a long way to illustrate current state vs desired state. And I think even more important than this is what the true cost will be if things stay the same.

This exercise begins with a basic consensus on value to demonstrate costs vs benefits. The simplest definition of what we mean by value is the equation everyone in any exchange carries in their heads either consciously or subconsciously:

> Value = Benefits − Costs
>
> or
>
> V = B − C

It's the way we can determine if relationships are one-sided or if there's give and take. It's an equation that can help determine fairness and soundness in decision making.

We also just know when there is more to lose than gain and vice versa without doing any calculations. But, when we add some quantifiers to the mix, that value gets real, really fast. Especially for 'transactions' or exchanges that are provider/customer ones – just not external customers who pay us money in exchange for services.

To demonstrate to leaders that keeping things as they are now is not in the best interests of the company, I'm suggesting you illustrate both scenarios: the first with an obvious external customer where the measurable value is more obvious; the second with an internal customer where measurable value is obscured and hidden. In both cases, you will be able to at the very least loosen the leader's grip on keeping the current ways of working in place.

HOW WE MEASURE VALUE

Value	Perceived value	Real value
Benefits: (profit, ROI, sales, efficiencies, ease)	(Benefits + Benefits + Benefits)	Perceived value x
−	−	Relevance
Cost: (time, effort, travel, wages)	(Cost + Risk)	

SCENARIO 1: EXTERNAL CUSTOMER

Make the activity one that is relevant to your company situation. If you produce or sell goods, make the scenario about that. If you sell services, make it about that or it will lose its meaning.

I'm going to use Steve's scenario to illustrate how decisions affect the external customer in a number of short- and long-term ways.

Start with the situation

(You can use the one I'll describe here as a guide to finding one of your own.)

Steve's company is a global manufacturer of cleaning equipment. Most of the machines are made overseas in Europe and are known to be the best in class in the industry. For decades now, the offer has been one based on quality over price. Of longevity over replacement. Of best results vs average. The company has enjoyed market dominance, and its sales team has for the most part been long-term veterans who are known and trusted by the customers in their portfolios.

Cite the challenge being faced

The sales team has been achieving targets in spite of an ever-tightening market. However, the company wants to go from $700m to $1b globally. The shareholders are demanding greater revenue from the sales team regardless of the methods used.

The Australian MD is passing on a target of $x which is a x% increase YOY. In addition to this, it's pushing for its team to now sell a cheaper line of product to a market they normally wouldn't sell to that cannibalises its existing market.

Lay out the impacts

Customers:

Trust is being eroded as existing, long-term customers are asking why they've been sold a more expensive product if the cheaper one is just as good. They are choosing to not renew leases on those items, and instead of replacing machines are choosing to just get them repaired.

Meanwhile, customers who are price driven and formerly not a 'traditional customer' of the company are being approached in a highly competitive market. It's a volume sell, low margin, and a lot of these machines must be sold to hit target.

Salespeople:

Some salespeople are leaving because they can no longer risk their personal reputation with people they've been doing business with, in some cases, for decades. They have lost faith in the direction of the company and don't believe in a cheap sell over the high-quality products they've successfully been selling for years.

Once belief is eroded in any salesperson, their ability to sell effectively is greatly diminished.

Commercial:

Cost of Sale and Customer Acquisition Cost: More activity is required to get to the new prospects – more visits, more travel, more time.

Margin: Margin on new products is significantly less because it's more of a volume product.

Cost to serve: Given that it's a cheaper product, it is likely to break down sooner and be out of action more frequently, causing customers to complain and call in for replacements or to fix the machinery. It will cause an increase in engage-ment across the business, such as accounts potentially not being paid until machines are replaced or fixed, supply chain delays in replacing machines from Europe could cause lags in payment even longer, services of local mechanics will be increasingly needed to fix issues onsite, customer service calls increase, calls to salespeople will go up from these customers, meaning less time for the higher value, loyal, higher margin customers.

Future revenue: Longer term customers will choose not to renew contracts and could choose to buy elsewhere. Revenue will diminish over time in a way that cannot be easily recovered.

Salespeople will leave, meaning fewer salespeople will be left to generate the same revenue. Less available funds to afford top talent: peanuts and monkeys.

Future profit: Ditto.

Now outline the potential solution with the Sales Revolution

1. CEO is a trusted adviser to shareholders instead of a mere order taker. This could mean a number of actions would be different, including:

    - asking questions to qualify the urgency and rationale behind the increase in revenue

    - unpacking the commercial reality if this is implemented

    - exploring the possibility of rolling out a longer term strategy alongside the current one, using a different inside sales model to create demand in new markets (lower cost of sale and lower customer acquisition cost) without cannibalising long-term customers

- outlining the potential for offering additional services to the long-term market that could increase revenue

- demonstrating a willingness to ask the global office for support in providing more machinery in stock to create a competitive advantage with lower-priced machines

- clarifying the post-purchase support differences between two ranges to highlight value differentiation

- highlighting the impact of the proposal on revenue, cost to serve, customer acquisition cost, margin, future revenue, salespeople, and profit, while weighing the costs of their demands against the benefits of a slightly different approach

- ensuring salespeople feel confident they can offer more to current customers without risking their credibility by providing a clear product value differential to customers.

2. Global supply chain: sees Australian market as a customer they value and therefore wants to support. Works together on commercial terms to supply product to timeframes.

3. MD understands the value experienced salespeople bring the company and can communicate that to shareholders and ELT to support them differently. Greater support for salespeople means experience is kept in the business, sales profitability is upheld and, in many cases, productivity is gained.

4. Marketing, sales (inside and field) and customer service work together to share insights from and to the market that drive greater share of wallet, new revenue opportunities and referrals.

5. By treating the shareholders like customers who matter, the MD is educating stakeholders about an even better scenario for them that isn't a sugar hit and won't devastate their future earnings. By educating shareholders, the MD gains credibility. Should the board decide to go ahead anyway, at least the MD has outlined the likely scenarios they can expect.

Don't mistake me here: managing directors have a very tough time with boards. Many are more concerned with keeping their jobs than they are with the harder job of challenging the board's or shareholders' wants. Many don't really understand the impact downstream of what they're asking and many – once that is explained to them – will understand and, in self-interest, want the better result for themselves. Shareholders won't become altruistic. It is their own self-interest though that is at stake by getting their own way without challenge. Managing both 'customers' – shareholders and the company's people – is the straddle. That's actually the job. However, short terms can result in short-term decisions.

SCENARIO 2: INTERNAL CUSTOMER

This is what distinguishes The Sales Revolution from any other 'sales' or 'customer centric' model. That's because of the broader definition of customer which we'll dive into in part III.

By changing the behaviour of every employee towards their customers (some will be internal), and getting to a measure of value to be delivered and then measuring the impact of what was delivered, a Culture of Customer™ becomes a way of being. Moreover though, the real measures of benefit or cost of decision making that would otherwise remain hidden becomes visible. **Accountability goes up when real impact is 'seen' because it's the truth.** It helps future decision making, future policy and process determination, and return on time invested starts to improve. It changes the way everyone thinks about how they do what they do. It stops siloed thinking and behaviour.

When we talk about internal service providers I mean functions like finance that produce reports to leaders in the business, or HR who provide advice to leaders about employees, or talent who recruit new people into the organisation. I'm talking about marketing who supports sales in the messaging to customers and who supports the company to generate greater market awareness of the brand and its products and services. Or people in administration that make the lives of those they work with easier by allowing them to focus on core tasks which generate a higher return. In the case of an Executive Assistant, however, it's almost like creating a double for the MD/CEO as they often sit in on and represent them when they need to be elsewhere so they can essentially be in two places at once. But the real value of all of these internal service provisions is for the most part understood in principle but hidden. And when something goes wrong, the cost is also hidden. Even when it doesn't go wrong but there is order-taking behaviour by internal service providers to their internal customers, there will be diminished value returned, if not higher cost incurred. Again, because it's not measured or communicated specifically, accountability is low and value is too.

The Sales Revolution changes this.

Again, start with the situation

Let's take the recruitment of a new salesperson, for example. A sales director asks HR to find them someone to look after a key territory that has been vacant for months now. The Sales Director gives HR a brief and HR without asking any questions uses a generic position description it has for the role, and engages a search firm.

Cite the challenge being faced

Because that territory has had no dedicated salesperson on it for months (and this territory has had two different salespeople in three years), it's hard to know how much of that portfolio's customer base has been eroded out of lack of service or because they've been exposed to competitors. The longer it remains unattended, the more revenue we have to lose. It's also unknown as to why this particular territory has had a turnover of people 50% higher than any other in the region.

Lay out the impacts

Customers:

Each time a new salesperson goes into the territory, customers are alerted to the fact that something must be wrong. Without the facts they make up stories that the manager must be toxic, the company doesn't pay well, or they don't recruit the right people. Regardless, it's not doing anything to build trust or make customers feel like they can open up in the same way they would with someone who they felt was going to be there to see the longer term impact of the decisions made from taking up services from them.

Some customers may have already switched to providers who – while maybe not as good – are more reliable, have more credibility simply as a result of being constant and consistent, and therefore they have greater confidence in.

Word of mouth is stopping others from wanting to leave their incumbents: why would I leave my current provider to go with someone who might not be there in 6 or 12 months?

Salespeople:

Potential candidates asking about who has been successful in the role before become dubious when they discover it's been a hard territory to fill and keep filled. They wonder why that is, and assume the territory must be a difficult one, or that there is something about the way the company operates that must be causing others to leave. Potentially great candidates are choosing not to take the role and some don't even continue in the recruitment process.

Other more desperate ones with less successful track records or less experience still move forward in the process or accept the role. This lack of experience or track record combined with a belief that the territory may be a tough one is causing them to underestimate the demands of the territory; they become frustrated by a lack of traction and success and end up leaving as well.

Commercial:

Cost of Sale and Customer Acquisition Cost: Every time a new person is recruited it adds to the cost of sale. It takes less experienced salespeople longer to convert new business which adds to the CAC.

Margin: Less experienced salespeople can discount to get a sale which diminishes margin. Less experienced salespeople miss opportunities to improve margin.

Cost to serve: Customers without a dedicated salesperson may call parts of the business more frequently when they have an issue – customer service, distribution or even finance. They may delay paying invoices because they feel it gets someone to call them or they feel invisible to the company.

Future revenue: Longer term customers will choose not to renew contracts and could choose to buy elsewhere. Revenue will diminish over time in a way that may not be easily recovered. Average sale and frequency of purchase can't be driven without a dedicated salesperson or resource.

Future profit: Profit is eroded through a combination of diminished revenue and increased costs.

Internal impact: It can cost more than what you initially think.

Before a hiring decision is even made, there are the additional costs internally that normally remain hidden. For example, consider the number of hours across each person involved in the process of going to market for a candidate and the recruitment agency fee.

In fact, before you even onboard this salesperson, the process itself has cost the business significant amounts of money – most of it absorbed by the business. Rarely is it measured. Rarely is the return weighed up against this measure of cost. But somewhere, someone in finance, someone in sales is doing the maths. They're doing the value equation in their heads and they're now adding in the risk. Risk of what? In short: of getting it wrong.

In a down market the risk of getting something wrong is very, very real.

So, what can go wrong and what is the cost of getting this new hire wrong?

Best case scenario of getting it wrong: we work out pretty quickly (in the first six weeks) it's not right and we let that person go within the probationary period. But even in such cases the cost is still significant, as shown in the table below. (My suggestion is to always be conservative on the numbers and base the salaries on very round numbers.)

COST OF GETTING A NEW SALES HIRE WRONG IN FIRST SIX WEEKS

Cost item	Total hours	Cost per hour	Item cost	Total
HR BP time	50	$63		$3150
Sales Director time	80	$80		$6400
Psychometric test			$300	$300
Placement fee			$18,000	$18,000
Salary of new hire			$12,000	$12,000
Time spent with new recruit by senior salesperson	60	$63		$3780
Travel costs:				$1500
Petrol			$600	
Tolls			$300	
Parking			$300	
Hospitality			$300	
Equipment costs:				$4400
Car lease			$1800	
Phone			$600	
Laptop			$2000	
Training costs			$2000	$2000
Total				$51,530

That's $51,530 in six weeks. Most of those costs are absorbed into the business. External costs are a bit more obvious. But unless that salesperson has generated $200,000 in new business in those six weeks, it's unlikely the return is enough to justify the risk. And what I've left out is where the cost really ramps up: that's in doing it all again. The only costs you don't need to replicate are the recruitment agency placement fee (as most will replace for no charge in certain timeframes) and the equipment costs (as they will be there for the next salesperson). The real risk is in the minds of the market where customers see a revolving door of salespeople:

> *Do we bother building a relationship here if they're going to leave or be let go of soon? What is wrong with the company if they can't find people who are a good fit? Are these people leaving or is the company letting them go? How come they didn't pick up that they weren't a fit during the recruitment phase or in checking references? Something mustn't be right there.*

And it's the same in the minds of other employees who might be asking similar questions. They're the risks we don't think about, and if we do, they are very tricky to measure the impact of. We just know there's a risk. We think the risk is just of getting it wrong and needing to go back out to market to do it all again. That's still significant.

Now show what the difference might be to that risk using The Sales Revolution

What if the approach was entirely different?

What if we mitigated the risk of getting it wrong by including the very people where there is the greatest risk of getting it wrong with in the vetting and onboarding processes? It's of course predicated on the fact that there must already be a strong Culture of Customer™ in the business where the line between 'customer' and business is dotted from a belonging perspective.

Cost item	Total hours	Cost per hour	Item cost	Total
HR BP time	50	$63		$3150
Sales Director time	50	$80		$4000
Psychometric test			$300	$300
Placement fee			$18,000	$18,000
Salary of new hire			$12,000	$12,000
Time spent with new recruit by:	20	$63		$1260
senior salesperson				
key supplier				
2 key customers				
Travel costs:				$300
hospitality			$300	
Equipment costs:				$2600
phone			$600	
laptop			$2000	
Training costs			$2000	$2000
Total				$43,610

It's not the $8000 saving that is significant here: it's the mitigation of the perceived risk by key customers and suppliers. When they're involved in the 'vetting' process, you get their buy in or out more strongly, waste less time continuing if they're not engaged with the prospective salesperson, and could save an additional $36,000 in placement fees.

This is why creating a strong Customer Consciousness™ and Culture of Customer™ has long-term measurable value for the business: not just in cost savings and avoidance of the cost of risk involved in decision making, but also in the value of bring-ing in those in your ecosystem close. By treating them like customers that matter (because they do), they get a say in the selection of the person they'll be seeing a lot of. It shows them their opinion matters to you, which can mean not just better retention numbers but the lifetime value of a customer goes up when they are loyal to you because they belong. The difference in two years compared to five years. The difference of five years to seven years and of seven to ten years. Then there is the addi-tional value of them referring new business to you.

HOW TO REDUCE THE COST OF CUSTOMER ACQUISITION[6]

Contributors to customer acquisition cost (CAC)	What increases CAC	What reduces CAC
Number of meetings per prospective customer	More meetings (lack of planning, ineffective execution, inability to build trust quickly)	Fewer meetings (able to progress conversation quickly, better questions, better research/preparation, influence skills, trust-building skills)
Conversion rate of visits into opportunities	Low conversion rate (lack of sales execution skills)	High conversion rate (high degree of sales execution skills)
Conversion rate of visits to proposals	Low conversion rate (lack of ability to deal with concerns, inability to make a compelling case)	High conversion rate (ability to deal with concerns and make a compelling case)
Time from conversion to invoice (days)	More days (lack of reinforcement of decision to buy)	Fewer days (ability to reinforce decision to buy)

---

6   To reduce the Customer Acquisition Cost, there needs to be work done on the skills that improve the ability of the sales team to affect the contributors. Low skill and consistency = Higher CAC. Better skill and consistency = Lower CAC.

LIFETIME VALUE OF A CUSTOMER

	Average customer spend	Frequency of purchase: Weekly Monthly Once off Ad hoc	Retention of customer Number of years	Number of additional revenue opportunities: Project work Additional opportunities in other areas of customer business Referrals
Inputs	Ability to value add/upsell	Trust Communication of value	Trust Emotional value Measurable delivery of value	Strength of relationships Understanding of business Feeling of belonging

BUT WAIT, THERE'S MORE ...

I have stuck here to sales and salespeople from a more internal perspective to illustrate how having a Customer Consciousness™ combined with Commercial Competence delivers measurable value to the business. But what about a non-sales example where an internal service provider is able to demonstrate the value they deliver to the business?

I'll use an example I cited in part I where a client of mine was having issues with their HR business partner team's perception internally. Many had not long graduated and were in their second role there. Now, just because they're young doesn't mean that they're not great at what they do, nor does it mean they don't know their stuff. They themselves weren't as confident as they should have been about the value they were delivering to some of their leaders, and the leaders couldn't see the value they were delivering also. And the business had no way of understanding the measure of value provided to the business by way of costs saved and productivity improved.

The Head of People and Culture was also aware that the real issue was a lack of skill in the HR Business Partners being able to diagnose the 'root cause' of the leaders' issues and, therefore, not just 'accept' on face value what the leader was telling them and putting together a solution based only on that (which is, folks, as we know, order taker behaviour), but on building a solution that provides a more permanent 'fix', builds leadership capability, and costs the business less either in the short or long term (and sometimes both).

By giving this team access to the same skills as the sales team, such as the ability to diagnose the real issue or get to the root cause of the problem being presented rather than 'order take' or just treat the symptom that is evident, they're able to solve the problem by addressing the root cause of it properly, and save the company money in more ways than one.

Nothing like a tight economy to drive the urgency. The time is ripe for such discussions.

CHAPTER 10

MORE ARTILLERY

UNCOVERING THE SIZE AND IMPACT OF THE PROBLEM

The scenario approach might work with some companies and leaders, but you may need additional artillery or a different approach entirely. When you manage to get the leaders together or even if you meet with them individually, here are some questions you may want to present and then unpack the answers to:

1   If sales targets are achieved how likely are you to actively look further into how they're being achieved?

2   If sales targets are achieved, how likely is it that a deeper dive into cost of sale or cost to serve will be evaluated?

3   How likely is it for new customers to be referred to your business by:

- a competitor?

- a supplier?

- an employee?

- another customer?

4   If customers leave, how likely are you to look beyond sales to identify the contributing factors?

5   How likely is it that more than 50% of the organisation knows who their customer is – including those in non-customer facing roles?

6   If asked, how likely is it that your (add and subtract as it relates to your business):

- Customer service team is able to tell you who their internal customer is?

    Are they able to articulate what matters to that customer?

    Tell you how to measure value they've delivered to that customer?

- Accounts team is able to tell you who their internal customer is?

    Are they able to articulate what matters to that customer?

    Tell you how to measure value they've delivered to that customer?

- Finance team is able to tell you who their internal customer is?

    Are they able to articulate what matters to that customer?

    Tell you how to measure value they've delivered to that customer?

- HR/People and Culture team is able to tell you who their internal customer is?

    Are they able to articulate what matters to that customer?

    Tell you how to measure value they've delivered to that customer?

- IT team is able to tell you who their internal customer is?

  Are they able to articulate what matters to that customer?

  Tell you how to measure value they've delivered to that customer?

- Warehouse team is able to tell you who their internal customer is?

  Are they able to articulate what matters to that customer?

  Tell you how to measure value they've delivered to that customer?

- Distribution team is able to tell you who their internal customer is?

  Are they able to articulate what matters to that customer?

  Tell you how to measure value they've delivered to that customer?

- Marketing team is able to tell you who their internal customer is?

  Are they able to articulate what matters to that customer?

  Tell you how to measure value they've delivered to that customer?

7   If salespeople give you feedback that other areas of the business are causing issues that affect customers' experiences with your company, how likely are you to:

- investigate further?

- take action that fixes the issue/s permanently?

- think salespeople are making excuses for non-performance?

8   When a salesperson leaves your business how likely are you to look beyond the sales function or sales leader for other contributing factors? Have you calculated the cost to the business each time this happens? How do you do that?

9

If these internal service providers aren't able to ...	How likely is it that it's ...
HR Business Partners Diagnose the real problem they're solving	**Costing the business significant amounts of money in:** · wages · recruitment fees · redundancies · wasted time · loss of talent · staff turnover · lost productivity
IT Fix issues quickly Enable teams to access technology that makes their roles more effective	**Costing the business money in:** · lost productivity · wasted time · staff turnover
Learning and Development Demonstrate how their programs are aligned with current and future skill and capability gaps Measure the impact of the value delivered	**Costing the business money in:** · time spent recruiting talent that has those skills · people not attending programs · programs not being run · people not being trained · people not attending programs

If these functions that interact with customers aren't able to …	How likely is it that it's …
Finance Get new customers set up quickly with trading terms Get invoices paid on time consistently Make payment of invoices easy for customers	Preventing revenue from being generated sooner Impacting cashflow Impacting revenue and cashflow
Marketing Speak to the issues customers want solved	Wasting money on campaigns that don't work Cost the business money in: • wages • wasted time • lost productivity
Customer Service Make the customer feel listened to, understood and heard Resolve an issue and ensure the root cause of that issue is fixed Communicate with the sales team about customer issues	Cost the business money in: • lost customers • lost revenue • time and wages when issues are escalated • time spent resolving the same issue • lost sales growth
Logistics Turn around a delivery in a timely manner Escalate deliveries for customers at risk Be responsive to internal customers who need support Go the extra mile with identified customers	Cost the business money in: • lost time • opportunity cost of time wasted • lost customers • lost revenue • fewer customer referrals

This will get you started. And it sure will get the conversation started.

Help your leadership team to start to get a measure of the impact of not doing these things first. The size of the problem and the impact of the size of the problem is a good starting point.

PART III

GETTING STARTED

Some say that we humans are each born with a soul. It's a part of us but not part of our physical reality. When we are connected to someone in the moment, our soul is awake. When we watch a sunset, our soul is alive. When a loved one passes, our soul grieves. It's the connection between the physical and the spiritual and has nothing to do with religion.

Can a business have a soul? Well, as Glen Simpson said:

> It took me a long time to realise in the business world, we tend to think of organisations and companies as entities. They're not, they don't exist. They are people, and the quality of the work they do and the productivity one gets out of working with or for them is totally dependent on how the people in that entity feel. And so if they believe in the company, if they believe in the purpose and they are supportive of a team, then it will achieve great things. So every time you see a person in an organisation, what you're seeing is the potential of that organisation. Your asset, your biggest asset steps out of the lift every morning when they come to work, and depending on how they feel in that moment will be the quality of your organisation and your outputs.

In other words, the soul of any company lies in the collective souls of its people. Our business soul comprises the people who work in our business, and within each person lies the potential of our company.

I find this sobering – especially in a tight market.

When you look at your people, how much potential lies dormant?

The Sales Revolution works to awaken the potential of every person in your company –transforming it from within as each person embarks on their own journey of transformation. It's not magic. But it is a completely different way of operating.

Surrounding our company in the business ecosystem can be supply partners, channel partners, distributors, franchisors, franchisees, referrers, the community ... How much potential there too lies dormant to us? When we have Mutual

Enrichment™ as a result of how we engage with one another, we awaken that potential too.

The problem is that most of us never give this much thought. We simply don't even think about the potential the people in our business world have, which means your company is unable to become fully realised. Our role is therefore to unlock this by discovering what matters most to each 'customer' and then delivering it.

A Culture of Customer™ is an inside-out job. The Sales Revolution methodology ensures that delivering value becomes your company's way of being. The customer will belong to the company and not to any one person or team alone. That's powerful.

And it's why understanding what matters to our customers can't simply be a CRM 'task' or 'stage'. That's why traditional sales models miss the heart of the issue.

The Sales Revolution is a transformation of effective behaviour executed consistently by everyone.

When customers know they matter because they do, they also know they belong. When I matter as much to you as you do to me there is Mutual Mattering™.

Does that mean that Jonesy in tech needs to become a salesperson?

Of course not.

But he does need to know his own internal customers and deliver measurable value to them. He must understand how his output helps the company deliver measurable value to the customers who pay us money.

Otherwise he's operating in a vacuum. He may well be creating some spectacular technologies but if no one uses them because they don't help someone achieve their top goals or solve their top challenges, they're irrelevant. And without relevance, there is no value.

You may know your company needs The Sales Revolution, but knowing and doing are two different beasts.

In part II, we got your leaders on board. This part gives you ways to get started. I promise it will be one of the most rewarding changes your business will make.

When customers (internal and external) know they matter to the business because they do, they stay.

They spend more.

They're more productive,

They contribute for the love of it.

They refer others.

They develop a deep skillset.

They're enriched by belonging to something bigger than themselves.

In this section we'll explore how to define customers, the critical role of leaders as models of excellence, why sales needs to reclaim its backbone, and how to spread mattering awareness across the business and into your business ecosystem and become part of your community again as a generous citizen.

CHAPTER 11

A NEW DEFINITION OF 'CUSTOMER'

CREATING CUSTOMER CONSCIOUSNESS™

Your business neither operates in a vacuum nor is impervious to others' behaviour.

Everything we do matters.

How one part of the business treats a customer will impact (positively or negatively) another part of the business. And the business itself of course.

This is why I am a champion for a company-wide education program of Customer Consciousness™. When that happens, decisions and actions are taken from a shifted perspective: one that's more well-rounded and more considered because the whole impact is better understood.

THE CULTURE OF CUSTOMER MODEL™

To create Customer Consciousness™, it's helpful to start with a definition of 'customer'. Now, if you or I asked any salesperson: 'What is a customer?' we'd likely get a range of responses like:

- 'Someone who buys from me.'

- 'Someone who comes into our store.'

- 'Someone who buys from our online store.'

- 'Anyone who pays us money in exchange for a good or service'.

Every now and then we might hear someone say:

- 'A friend.'

- 'Someone I have a commercial relationship with.'

- 'Anyone I work with.'

Rarely would we hear customers defined as:

- the company itself

- our leaders

- my team and colleagues

- my direct reports

- the supply chain

- the value chain

- the wider business ecosystem

- the community the business operates within

My definition of a 'customer' is:

> Anyone with whom we deliver measurable value to by doing our role.

And before you tell me, I acknowledge ladies and gentlemen that mine is indeed a wide brushstroke of a definition! ☺

Deliberately!

If we define a customer only as the person or company that buys a product or service from us, we are limited. That definition narrows our thinking and therefore our approach towards revenue generation, margin improvement, how each person contributes to the profitable growth of the company, and the way we deliver value to those we work with in that pursuit.

I think it misses the much bigger picture.

If we limit our understanding and definition of 'customer', we also risk being stuck forever in the past, wondering why we're running very fast only to stay still.

CHAPTER 12

LEADERS FIRST

The fact that you're reading this book tells me you really want to make a difference in your business. Regardless of whether it's your own business or simply one you work for, you clearly care a great deal. Here are some ways to start to take direct action in a straightforward way.

You may be the person in your company who creates awareness of the need to change.

My methods are tried and tested.

And they're pretty simple to implement once everyone is on board.

CREATE CUSTOMER CONSCIOUSNESS™ WITH LEADERS FIRST

You must start with the leaders in your business.

When leaders understand the concept of Customer Consciousness™, they can be the models of excellence that lead their teams into that new way of operating. Leaders must first understand who *their* customers are, and then *why* it's important to uncover what matters most to those customers to deliver measurable value to them.

When leaders adopt Customer Conscious behaviours with their own customers, it enables a team-by-team experience of immersion in Customer Consciousness™. The teams experience what it feels like as a *customer who matters*. Immersion makes it easier for those team members to then take a similar approach with their own customers.

The three activities I'm going to outline for you in this chapter to use with your leadership team use the Growth Model™ to take them through these stages:

1   Awareness that they have customers, and who those customers are.

2   Accountability to one another in their leadership group by reporting the measure of value delivered to those customers.

3   Acting purposefully to uncover what matters to those customers, and then delivering measurable value to them.

4   Acceptance that value is exchanged with those customers.

Book a meeting room and invite all the senior leadership team to take part in an information session for an hour. The following activities can all be undertaken in that timeframe with you facilitating.

THE GROWTH MODEL™

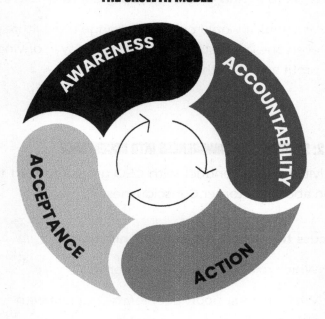

ACTIVITY 1: BEGIN TO CREATE AWARENESS

Start with the following activity that allows them to 'drop into' the concept that your company needs to do something differently by highlighting obvious things that aren't working right now, *and* getting their buy in.

> **Raise your hand if you relate to any of these ...**
>
> - It's getting harder to find great people who 'get' that the customer is the reason for our business (regardless of their role).
>
> - Your sales team (or you) is succeeding at new customer acquisition, but starting to lose customers because of a poor experience elsewhere in the business.

- It's hard to find, let alone keep, great sales talent.

- You think it would positively change the culture if everyone understood the role they play in driving profit and growth.

ACTIVITY 2: SHIFTING FROM AWARENESS INTO ACCEPTANCE

This activity is one I conduct with CEO groups to start the conversation about Customer Consciousness™.

Discuss the people in your organisation

- Which roles interact with customers?

- Which roles support people who interact with customers?

- Which roles don't realise they interact with customers?

- How about your executive team?

- How customer-oriented are they?

- How well does the executive team align their functions/teams into a relationship that really matters to your customers?

ACTIVITY 3: INTO ACTION: DO A DEEP DIVE ON THE CEO'S CUSTOMERS

While many of you will have facilitated meetings before, this activity may be a stretch as it requires you to paint a picture for the leaders and take them on a bit of a journey.

These are my words of course, but you can use the gist of what I'm saying in your own way to make it relevant to your own leadership team ...

As leaders in this business you have many 'customers'. You may choose to call them 'stakeholders' but regardless of the name, they're people and entities you need to deliver value to. There is undoubtedly a relationship between you and those people or entities. And that relationship is contingent on more than simply the value you deliver. That's because how we deliver that value is also 'of value'.

To be more specific, let's say I'm the CEO.

Here is a table of my 'customers', along with what I may have uncovered through a number of insight-building conversations with them to discover what matters most to them, why it matters most and how they measure that value delivered.

CUSTOMERS WHO MATTER TO THE CEO

Customer role	What matters most to them	What success looks like for them from our working relationship
Executive Assistant	Understand the CEO's top priorities and those of the executive team Organisational direction, strategy and goals for next 12 months Clear communication of expectations and timeframes	Being trusted to stand in for CEO because I understand her priorities and strategic direction and approach Helping CEO achieve big wins for organisation
The company	Revenue goals Profit goals Attraction and retention of best talent Attraction and retention of best customers	Happy employees who are more productive because they love what they do (return on capital) Happy employees who stay more than the average of two years Customers who are aligned with our values and stay because they love the experience
The board	Shareholder return increases Profit improvements Long-term strategic direction that ensures business is set up to grow in spite of market challenges	Board confidence in CEO's direction and decision making
The leadership team	Clarity over strategic direction of business and focus for functional areas Acknowledgement of success and contribution to strategic targets Opportunity to grow professionally Opportunity to grow team capability	Support for initiatives that facilitate the strategic goals of the business Training for team members to enable them to achieve what is required of them Feeling of being a team that is headed in the same direction

Customer role	What matters most to them	What success looks like for them from our working relationship
My direct reports	Clarity over success measures and timeframes	Acknowledgement of contribution to strategic goals
	Feedback on progress in order to course correct or confirm approach	Ability to attend professional development programs.
	Opportunities to grow professionally	Regular one on ones that ensure I'm on track
The end customers	Value from services rendered	Knowing that everyone I speak with in the company is on the same page when we communicate (that they all know what matters to me and deliver that, no matter who it is)
	Feeling like I belong to company	
	Reward for loyalty	
		Better outcomes that I know I can only get by working with this company
The media	Insight into company's culture and decision making	Direct access to CEO
	Stories that are useful to them	Direct quotes from CEO
	Regular communication	
Our suppliers	Understanding our strategic direction and goals	Referrals from us
	Long-term relationships	Close collaboration to ensure ongoing trade
		Contract renewals
The community	Clarity over what we do and how we bring our expertise to the community to benefit locals	We care about more than just our paying customers and shareholders: we give back to them in meaningful ways
	Ability to participate in our programs	

I've kept them general because they're made up ☺.

If however I wanted this to be actual, it would be important for me as the CEO (or anybody who genuinely wants to deliver value to each customer) to get an actual measure of value to be clear for both about what success looks like: the difference made as a direct result of the value exchange.

If we did get a measure of value and applied it to each customer, what might it look like? Let's add another column to our table to find out.

MEASURE OF VALUE TO CUSTOMERS WHO MATTER TO CEO

Customer role	What matters most to them	What success looks like for them from our working relationship	Value measure
Executive Assistant	Understand the CEO's top priorities and those of the executive team Organisational direction, strategy and goals for next 12 months Clear communication of expectations and timeframes	Being trusted to stand in for CEO because I understand her priorities and strategic direction and approach Helping CEO achieve big wins for organisation	Number of meetings EA goes to on behalf of CEO with ELT or board Number of projects involved with that deliver strategic outcomes and measure of those outcomes
The company	Revenue goals Profit goals Attraction and retention of best talent Attraction and retention of best customers	Happy employees who are more productive because they love what they do (return on capital) Happy employees who stay more than the average of two years Customers who are aligned with our values and stay because they love the experience	Return on capital YOY retention rates or average tenure Customer retention rates since a particular strategic decision or year

Customer role	What matters most to them	What success looks like for them from our working relationship	Value measure
The board	Shareholder return increases	Board confidence in CEO's direction and decision making	Positive votes by the board
	Profit improvements		Retention rate of CEO
	Long-term strategic direction that ensures business is set up to grow in spite of market challenges		Percentage of board in favour of CEO strategies
The leadership team	Clarity over strategic direction of business and focus for functional areas	Support for initiatives that facilitate the strategic goals of the business	Measure of impact each functional area has had on relevant strategic goals
	Acknowledgement of success and contribution to strategic targets	Training for team members to enable them to achieve what is required of them	Percentage improvement rate of an outcome since training
	Opportunity to grow professionally	Feeling of being a team that is headed in the same direction	360-degree survey results
	Opportunity to grow team capability		
My direct reports	Clarity over success measures and timeframes	Acknowledgement of contribution to strategic goals	Number of times individuals have been publicly and privately acknowledged for specific contribution and impact it made
	Feedback on progress in order to course correct or confirm approach	Ability to attend professional development programs.	Percentage of DRs provided with PD
	Opportunities to grow professionally	Regular one on ones that ensure I'm on track	Percentage of DRs with ongoing consistent one-on-one meetings with CEO
			Percentage of one-on-ones that are maintained

Customer role	What matters most to them	What success looks like for them from our working relationship	Value measure
The end customers	Value from services rendered Feeling like I belong to company Reward for loyalty	Knowing that everyone I speak with in the company is on the same page when we communicate (that they all know what matters to me and deliver that, no matter who it is) Better outcomes that I know I can only get by working with this company	Customer surveys Customer testimonials Customer retention rates Measures of value delivered with customer
The media	Insight into company's culture and decision making Stories that are useful to them Regular communication	Direct access to CEO Direct quotes from CEO	Percentage increase in favourable articles No. scheduled phone calls or meetings per quarter
Our suppliers	Understanding our strategic direction and goals Long-term relationships	Referrals from us Close collaboration to ensure ongoing trade Contract renewals	Dolar value of new business from our referrals to them Continuity of revenue from us
The community	Clarity over what we do and how we bring our expertise to the community to benefit locals Ability to participate in our programs	We care about more than just our paying customers and shareholders: we give back to them in meaningful ways	Measurable personal impact as a result of company initiative

ACCOUNTABILITY: GETTING TO A MEASURE OF VALUE IS WHERE THINGS START TO CHANGE

It enables accountability because there is tangible evidence of value delivered. It adds Commercial Competence to Customer Consciousness™ with clear business outcomes.

Unseen becomes seen.

Intangible becomes tangible.

Dots can more easily be connected between action and impact.

Without this, it's too easy for Customer Consciousness™ to be a 'desirable' thing to develop rather than something that improves outcomes for all. In a down market, this is especially important, but down market aside: it changes behaviour in a real and meaningful way because it can be measured and managed. And as the old saying goes: 'What gets measured gets managed, and what gets managed gets done.'

Everyone in the company will become very conversant with the **10 Measures of Commercial Competence** as a result of The Sales Revolution.[7] The way everyone delivers value to the company, the end customer and to their own customers becomes real and relevant. More than that though: what also becomes obvious is that the success of each role depends on others also being successful in their roles.

Measures matter.

---

7   The 10 Measures of Commercial Competence are covered in chapter 16.

CHAPTER 13

THE REST OF THE BUSINESS

We now turn to others in the company, because if everyone in the company is to have Customer Consciousness™, they must first understand who they serve (who their customers are). They must be able to then uncover what matters to their direct customers through eyeball-to-eyeball conversations.

The activities in chapter 12 can also be conducted with the rest of the business, team by team. Once completed, moving your company towards a Culture of Customer™ requires enabling everyone to understand and implement what will deliver value to their customers.

While this is relatively simple, even salespeople (who should be conversant with these concepts) often think they're psychic when it comes to knowing what their customers value and how they measure value delivered. Eyeball-to-eyeball conversations are necessary. It's what the customer tells us matters to them. It's not for us to make assumptions or guess – especially when we *think* we know.

When you ask people in your company what customers value, you may get responses like: 'Isn't it obvious? They want better rates for their [insert your product or service here] … it's all about price.'

Compound that with a tight market and suddenly all sales-people want to do is discount, without understanding the down-stream impact that has on margin and profit. And the point is – they are completely missing the point!

So if salespeople make assumptions about what matters to customers, we may need to accept that those in the company who *don't even know* they have a customer may need to be taken on a journey even to get to *that* point – let alone also understand that this is the equation we all have in our heads whenever we're the 'buyer' or 'customer'. We're weighing up value all the time:

Value (V) = Benefit (B) – Cost (C)

Value is often misunderstood. It's equated too often with just the price of the product or service customers buy.

ROME WASN'T BUILT IN A DAY

Getting everyone to have Customer Consciousness™ will take some effort and training.

If we want to see a different outcome, it's only fair we build the capacity of those we want to see different (better) outcomes from so they can actually deliver them.

To reshape the way everyone in the company treats their customers, a new set of skills is recommended. We will look at each of these over the next three chapters.

- Understanding the three types of value (chapter 14).

- Understanding how to uncover a measure of value (chapter 15).

- Understanding how to deliver value (chapter 16).

A NEW APPRECIATION OF VALUE

WHAT IS VALUE?

Let's say I'm a company considering a lead-generation supplier. The whole time I'm in a conversation with this supplier, I may have something resembling the below calculation going on in my mind:

Value =

Benefits (more leads, more prospective customers, without needing to hire someone to do this)

–

Costs (uncertainty about the impression or quality of those calls to prospective customers, hassle if it goes south)

And it's the weight these items have in my mind too. If the cost is perceived by me to be too high, the benefits, while solid, may not be enough for me to see value and therefore buy.

REAL VALUE

Value	Perceived value	Real value
Benefits: (profit, ROI, sales, efficiencies, ease)	(Benefits + Benefits + Benefits)	Perceived value x
–	–	Relevance
Cost: (time, effort, travel, wages)	(Cost + Risk)	

Whether we're delivering service externally to customers or internally to our colleagues, that same equation is going on inside the heads of the receivers of each 'service'.

Want to get noticed internally? Deliver more value than is expected.

Want to get a sale? Demonstrate more value through mitigating potential costs and dial up the benefits as they relate to the customer's priority issues.

It isn't hard.

And yet like most simple things, because it's easy to do it's also easy *not* to do.

Real value is a simple concept that can make a big difference when it's understood by everyone who is of service to others. Imagine it being included in every induction program your company does. That alone would start to shift the way we operate internally with greater productivity and externally with better sales outcomes and customer loyalty and retention.

UNDERSTANDING THE THREE TYPES OF VALUE

The way we understand value therefore requires a new and more comprehensive appreciation. If you don't already know the three different types of value, they are:

- financial value
- functional value
- emotional value.

Let's look at each, with some examples.

WHAT IS FINANCIAL VALUE?

Financial value is the return on a product or service rendered, measured in currency.

It can include:

- revenue
- sales
- improved margin
- reduced expenses
- return on investment, return on capital, return on expenses
- reduced cost to serve.

For example, through working with The Sales Doctor, Munchable Catering has been able to secure $3 million in new business as a direct result of applying the skills taught in the workshops.[8]

WHAT IS FUNCTIONAL VALUE?

Functional value is a reduction of friction, time or effort as a result of the product purchased or service rendered.

---

8   Not a real example! (Although this is exactly what can and does happen.)

Functional value delivery makes things easier and results happen faster.

It can include:

- reduction in hours spent on a task

- reduction in headcount

- reduction in days to sign contracts

- efficiency improvements

- reduction in lost freight

- reduction in accounting errors

- percentage increase of invoices paid on or before due date

- less red tape, meaning it's easier to convert customers on the spot.

Most functional value can be rolled up into a financial value measure.

For example, time saved can be measured through the value of that time and the opportunity cost of that time, such as faster turnaround time from order to delivery. The questions that will give a measure of functional value include:

- How much time has been saved?

- What is the value of that time?

- What is the average order value?

- How many more orders can be delivered in the same time now?

- What does that mean for revenue?

WHAT IS EMOTIONAL VALUE?

It's easy to assume that emotional value will be 'fluffy' and unmeasurable, which isn't true.

Emotional value is the measure of sentiment that results from the way the product purchased or services are rendered.

It includes things like:

- trust

- loyalty

- referrals

- culture improvement.

And it's measured in a variety of ways which again can mostly be rolled up into a financial value. I say 'mostly' because some measures are more difficult to tie to emotional value alone. Trust, for example, may produce better customer conversion rates, and improve customer and employee retention rates (especially when prices are increased or discounts end).

What may be harder to tie to emotional value is when things like productivity go up as a result of a stronger connection by employees to purpose, or reduced absenteeism or fewer sick days. Trust, loyalty and cultural improvement can be measured through 360-degree feedback surveys or external customer surveys.

* * *

EXAMPLES OF THE THREE TYPES OF VALUE

VALUE	=	BENEFITS	–	COSTS
FINANCIAL VALUE	=	FINANCIAL BENEFITS	–	FINANCIAL COSTS
($)		Revenue/sales		Delivery costs
		ROI/ROE/ROC		Manufacturing costs
		Improved margin		Marketing costs
		Profit		
		New leads		
FUNCTIONAL VALUE	=	FUNCTIONAL BENEFITS	–	FUNCTIONAL COSTS
Ease		Saves time/fast turnaround time		Difficult processes
Effort		Minimal steps to sign up		Time consuming
Time		One point of contact		Hard to work with
		Better reporting		Multiple points of contact
		Makes my job easier		
EMOTIONAL VALUE	=	EMOTIONAL BENEFITS	–	EMOTIONAL COSTS
Trust		Trusted adviser		Says one thing does another
Loyalty		Reliable		Treats me like a number/order
		Honest		Doesn't follow through
		Trusted expertise		Late
		Does what they say they'll do when they say they'll do it		
		On time		

The previous table shows some more examples.

Without knowing all three measures of value, it's easy to miss what is valuable to those you serve. Without knowing, you're guessing; and when you're guessing, your delivery of value will be hit and miss.

CHAPTER 15

DISCOVERING WHAT MATTERS MOST TO THOSE WHO MATTER MOST

Using similar activities, we used to ensure Awareness and Acceptance of customers, we arrive at the point where we need to have conversations with each of our 'customers' (or representative of that customer group) to uncover what matters and why those things matter to them to ascertain a measure of value to each.

CONVERSATION PLANS

RESHAPE

I use conversation plans to structure these as they enable us to use the Covey principle of 'starting with the end in mind' so we know what we want to walk away knowing or achieving by the end of each conversation. Then we can structure those conversations to best elicit what matters from each customer.

CONVERSATION PLANS TO DISCOVER WHAT MATTERS TO THOSE WHO MATTER

Background	What is the context? How much do we know already? Length of relationship, strength, etc.
Result	What outcome do we want by the end of the conversation? Must be written in a way that means we're able to answer 'yes we did achieve it' or 'no we didn't achieve it'.
Objectives	Two or three objectives that contribute to the achievement of the result.
Audience	Who are you meeting with? What are their drivers?
Key message	What do you want the person/team you're meeting with to walk away knowing, doing or feeling as a result of your time together?
How	How will you set the conversation up to achieve your objectives and result? This can look like an agenda (yours). While conversations aren't linear, it helps to structure your thinking with questions, sequence, introductions and setting up next steps.

So what would this look like for a conversation with a leader and their direct report?

In the following example, the Sales Director has the Business Development Manager reporting in to her.

There is a bit of history here, so in order to uncover what matters and get alignment, the Sales Director may create a conversation plan that resembles this one.

EXAMPLE OF A CONVERSATION PLAN WITH AN INTERNAL CUSTOMER

Background	Lauren is a top performer in terms of opportunity creation but lacks commercial acumen, is still transactional and has levelled out in closing deals with warehouse managers. She doesn't have a strategic approach which limits her in identifying, engaging and influencing more senior decision makers and key influencers in organisations which means when an opportunity stalls, she simply moves on. It's not a long-term solution. Lauren resists coaching support and the opportunity to invest in her own development which could be due to low confidence in front of her peers.
Result	To have her articulate the long-term and life benefits of building and rounding out her capacity with coaching as a professional, not just as a salesperson.
Objectives	To get Lauren to articulate that the program is not just about "selling": it's about becoming someone others listen to, act on advice from which goes beyond selling into life and career opportunities To get Lauren to make the link between having these skills and being a powerful woman in the industry To get her to agree that there is another level of engagement she can develop that gives her the runway into even more opportunities: sales, career, life.
Audience	Lauren: hubris, no real confidence. Without results or her currency in her role, may doubt her value.
Key message	Lauren is valued by the business as a person we want to invest in: she's worth it and she needs to grow with the business.
How	Thank you.
	In order to get on the same page, I wanted to talk with you today about why we care so much that you are a committed and active participant in the work we're doing with Ingrid and to see how you can make the connection beyond simply sales skills to your goal of being a powerful woman in the industry. Is that okay?
	You know better than most that selling skills are life skills is that fair to say? You mentioned early on in the program that you wanted to make a difference in the industry: to be a powerful voice. is that still important to you? So to make a difference, it helps to be someone who other people choose to listen to and someone who has skills that can influence into action executives through to warehouse managers. Does that make sense?
	Okay.
	How are the reasons for making decisions at warehouse level different to say a CFO or a COO? What makes you say that? Give me an example. Where we'd like you to be is someone who is a senior person at Tuco and someone who can make a difference in the way that they're able to engage a variety of people by understanding how to do that regardless of who is in front of them, which is why we'd like you to have an hour a month one on one with Ingrid. How does that sound?
	If you had greater influencing skills, the ability to present across levels in an organisation and a strategic approach to engagement, how could that set you up to make a difference in the industry?
	How prepared are you to grow with the business in that regard? We'd like that person to be you. If you did become that person of influence in the industry, how would that give you greater opportunities in general? How could it open up other doors for you? What do you need to do to get started?

There are a number of benefits to using conversation plans:

- They act as a self-coaching tool that assesses the success of each conversation: did I achieve my outcome? If I didn't achieve my outcome, where did I fall down? What do I need to do to fix it? What are the learnings? What is the next step? Or if they did achieve their outcome, the reflective questions may be along the lines of: how do I know? What specific examples tell me this? What do I need to do now? What new awarenesses do I now have as a result?

- They ensure you set your approach up in advance to prevent winging it and just having a 'happy chat'. While 'happy chats' may feel more comfortable, they usually don't achieve clarity over what matters and why, they waste your time and theirs, and they fail to enable you to know what action to take now to deliver what matters.

- They facilitate better relationships because they allow you to be fully present for your customer. They act as a mental rehearsal that engenders confidence. The heavy lifting is done prior by noting quality questions and talking points so your brain doesn't have to be 'creating the next question' while you're also listening.

- They deliver better outcomes in less time. When you're clear about where you want to land a conversation, it's easier to bring it back on track when the conversation meanders. It means you've chosen better questions to uncover the right information that is meaningful to you both. It values both of you by demonstrating thoughtful input into how you're asking and listening. Customers understand this and feel like they matter. In essence, when done well, conversation plans deliver emotional and functional value.

CHAPTER 16

DELIVERING VALUE TO THOSE WHO MATTER

CREATING A CULTURE OF CUSTOMER

The Sales Revolution is about delivering measurable value to every customer. When every person knows about the following 10 metrics that matter and the impact of each one across the business, we begin to enter into a Culture of Customer™.

The 10 Measures of Commercial Competence:

1   Revenue

2   Margin

3   Cost of sales

4   Customer acquisition cost

5   Lifetime customer value

6   Cost to serve

7   Return on time invested

8   Return on capital

9   Return on expense

10   Return on investment

THE IMPACT OF THE 10 MEASURES OF COMMERCIAL COMPETENCE ACROSS THE BUSINESS

Metric that matters	Impact across the business ecosystem when it increases	Impact across the business ecosystem when it decreases
Revenue	More is purchased from suppliers Resources can be spent on community causes New people can be hired Existing people may be paid more Increased footprint in the market Improved marketing to attract more customers Positive sentiment and optimism Attract new talent People are invested in	Headcount is reduced Costs are examined Recruitment freeze Price increases that place further pressure on sales to communicate to customers Restructure of roles Pressure on the sales team to deliver Increased scrutiny on numbers Investment is paused
Margin	Salespeople may be rewarded with bonuses or commissions Business growth	Greater scrutiny on how to improve it: productivity, resource allocation, capacity, pricing Downstream headcount reduction to reduce pressure on net profit Investment reduced to preserve profit Supplier relationships re-examined

Metric that matters	Impact across the business ecosystem when it increases	Impact across the business ecosystem when it decreases
Cost of 'sales'	Restructure of sales team	Better commercial terms can be delivered to customers
	Headcount reduction or salary cap/reduction for new hires = less experienced salespeople	More orders means more production, more marketing, more invoicing, more deliveries
	Sales can spiral down meaning less is purchased which affects orders, and other areas of the business	Increased recruitment numbers
	Greater scrutiny on individual performance	Sense of certainty across the business: increased employment applications
	Analysis of travel costs and budget reductions	Confident selling: faster conversions and higher conversion rates
	Fewer customers or less spend can mean a gradual headcount reduction internally in an effort to reduce the impact on net profit	Greater downstream demand
	Uncertainty in the business: may lose good people	
	Technology solutions sought	
'Customer' acquisition cost	Examination of sales skills and process	More budget to reinvest across the business
	Fewer customers seen: vulnerable to competitors	Growth potential
	Marketing spend reduced	
Lifetime 'customer' value	Profit increases	Profit reduced
	Revenue increases	Revenue impacted
	Growth	Shorter term decision making
	Footprint expanded	People leave: customers and employees
	New products/services created	Loss of experience, knowledge, expertise
	Investment across the business	
	Greater customer retention: includes employee retention	
	Net promoter score improvements	
	Cultural survey results improved	

Metric that matters	Impact across the business ecosystem when it increases	Impact across the business ecosystem when it decreases
Cost to serve	Profit increases	Profit reduced
	Revenue increases	Revenue impacted
	Growth	Shorter term decision making
	Footprint expanded	People leave: customers and employees
	New products/services created	
	Investment across the business	Loss of experience, knowledge, expertise
	Greater customer retention: includes employee retention	
	Net promoter score improvements	
	Cultural survey results improved	
Return on time invested	Greater confidence	Profit reduced
	Improved sentiment	Revenue impacted
Return on capital	Improved retention rates: customer and employee	Shorter term decision making
Return on expense		People leave: customers and employees
Return on investment	Reinvestment in professional development	Loss of experience, knowledge, expertise
	Growth investment	Reduce customer service, distribution, warehouse, headcount

EXAMPLES OF HOW EACH FUNCTION CAN IMPROVE THE 10 MEASURES OF COMMERCIAL COMPETENCE

Metric that matters	Sales	Marketing	Accounts	P&C	Customer service	Operations
Revenue	Increase sales: activity and effectiveness Create an experience that makes customers refer others	Increasing market awareness and demand	Experience with customers that makes it easier for customers to spend and pay on time	Improve quality of salespeople recruited and skills	Solve problems to retain customers	Simplifying processes to reduce obstacles to selling, buying and solving issues
Margin	Not discounting Selling on value not price	Reinforcing messages of value Customer Communication and belonging	Experience customers have with accounts	Improve quality of salespeople recruited and skills to maximise margin	Retained customers	Strategy aligned to quality over price Availability of product Reduced turnaround on product orders Improved supplier prices and terms
Cost of 'sales'	Improved ways of working Allocation of time to type of account Fewer meetings to convert new customers Mix of in-person and online conversations	Generating demand Educating customers Reduced sales cycles	Experience customers have with accounts Less paperwork Less red tape Easier customer onboarding	Improve quality of salespeople recruited and skills to maximise margin Policies that clarify expectations for salespeople Improved communication skills across the business	Experience that creates more customer referrals	Reduction of barriers to entry Improved processes Technology that supports better customer insights Improved supplier prices and terms

Metric that matters	Sales	Marketing	Accounts	P&C	Customer service	Operations
'Customer' acquisition cost	Improved ways of working Allocation of time to type of account Fewer meetings to convert new customers Mix of in-person and online conversations	Generating demand Educating customers Reduced sales cycles	Experience customers have with accounts Less paperwork Less red tape Easier customer onboarding	Improve quality of salespeople recruited and skills to maximise margin Policies that clarify expectations for salespeople	Experience that creates more customer referrals	Reduction of barriers to entry Improved processes Technology that supports better customer insights
Lifetime 'customer' value	Improved experience Mutual enrichment Aligned delivery Increased frequency and value of purchase Identification of new opportunities	Reinforce and reward loyalty Reinforce and reward referrals Make customer feel like they belong with dedicated programs	Ways to pay made easier Incentive for payment on time Rewards for loyalty: dollars to spend on other services	Improved quality of skills across the business	Experience that prioritises loyal customers Personalised service Pre-emptive service and Solutions Better communication with sales and operations to have improved customer oversight	Technology that improves proactive decision making and solution provision Easier ways of working Less red tape

Metric that matters	Sales	Marketing	Accounts	P&C	Customer service	Operations
Cost to serve	Not being afraid to challenge customer requests that would compromise profit Educating customers	Improving website experience to aid self-resolution of issues	Streamlined payment and invoicing Strong relationships with customer's accounts people	Education Improved skills HR policies that foster clarity about what good looks like Experienced, highly skills new hires	Experience that prioritises loyal customers Personalised service Pre-emptive service and Solutions First-call resolution	Technology that improves proactive decision making and solution provision Easier ways of working Less red tape Better supplier relationships
Return on time invested *Return on capital* *Return on expense* *Return on investment*	Shortened sales cycles Improved conversion rates Better planning and execution Clarity over pipeline Understanding total team expenses and contribution to cost reductions	Improved insight into internal and external customers Resolving real issue Solutions that deliver better business outcomes			Better communication with sales and operations to have improved customer oversight	Easy ways to measure Clarity on policies and procedures to reduce time investigating

TIME TO IMPLEMENT A PLAN

Just like we did with the leaders, once each team of peers has uncovered what matters and, ideally, how their customers will measure what matters, it's time to implement a plan that will deliver value to each of those customers.

Presenting that plan to a group of peers will create group accountability and public commitment. My suggestion is for each group to come back together once they've gone to each 'customer' to uncover what matters and present their findings to each other, using the following questions as an example of how to structure their presentation:

- What did they discover mattered to each of their customers and what was the measure of value for each one?

- When will they deliver value? What is the next step with each customer?

- How will they do this and how frequently?

- When will they know they've delivered that value to each customer?

- When will they report back to the group?

After delivering value, it's important to go back and get to a measure of value delivered with each customer so it becomes *real*. By real, I mean visible. And visible means there is accountability more publicly in a way that is understood not simply by the customer themselves but more widely by the company.

This sets a new standard in the business of accountability.

It is the truth.

Conducting the value delivered conversation requires a clear measure of value to have been uncovered in the first place. The solution agreed to with the customer means there is already accountability built into the process before circling back.

The value delivered conversation contains four key elements:

- Restating the problem to be solved, challenge to be overcome or goal to be achieved.

- Reviewing the (measured) impact the problem, challenge or unrealised goal was having for them in their role, and for the company.

- Review the solution in terms of key steps taken to implement it.

- As a result of the solution being implemented, what has been possible to achieve that otherwise wouldn't have happened? What is the difference it has made? What are they now able to do that without your solution they wouldn't have been able to do (get a measure)?

ESTABLISH ACCOUNTABILITY THROUGH PEER GROUPS

Accountability is key to creating a permanent shift in behaviour. Group accountability is powerful too, not only because there is public sharing of action to be taken (a verbal commitment which increases the likelihood that any subsequent action will be consistent with that), but because a follow up of progress, action implemented and measure of that action is established. This increases the likelihood of action being taken not once, but continually, and a record of value as a result of that action is calculated and publicly communicated.

CHAPTER 17

DON'T WAIT FOR THE TRUCK TO HIT YOU

RESHAPE

TAPS ON THE SHOULDER

When I was in my thirties (yes, a long time ago) I had my first business. I loved it with all my heart because it was my creation and it filled me.

I had purpose.

But I had no idea what I was doing, and even though I was good at selling and had plenty of customers, I didn't really know how to run a business. It was recommended to me that I seek out a business coach.

Which I did.

During my onboarding with that business coach, he showed me three images:

He said to me that if I didn't pay attention to the tap on the shoulder, life will hit me with the plank to see if that wakes me up, and if I still refused to pay attention the Mack Truck was inevitable. The problem with the Mack Truck is that most people don't get back up after being hit.

I thought I 'got' the lesson. I didn't think I was stupid. But I was about to learn the lesson directly because I had wilful blindness.

The more time passed and the more successful my business became, the more revenue and profit I earned (after three years my sales had increased by about 300%, my net profit by 174% and I was on my way to 20 permanent employees), the bigger my ego became. As my ego grew, so too did my lack of willingness to find the weak spots and fix them.

I wanted to coast, if I'm honest. And I was tired.

I'd love to say that in my mid-thirties I was enlightened. I probably fooled myself into thinking I was, but I'm pretty sure I became an arsehole.

Taps on the shoulder?

Sheesh – I didn't want to know about them!

The truth is I could see where improvements needed to be made but I brushed them aside. Instead of doing something differently or even simply paying attention to what was going on, I kept ploughing on – I just wished the problems weren't there. More than that: I complained about them being there while also refusing to fix them.

Of course, those taps became planks, and by the time year 10 rolled around I was inevitably hit by the Mack Truck that was the end of my business. I needed to close the doors and walk away.

My team hated me.

I hated me.

And I came to hate the business I had created with love.

The truth is it needn't have been this way. I wasn't paying attention to the signs that things were going wrong in my business – with my team, with my customers – and I'd lost touch with the numbers. I was burnt out. Instead of continuing to move forward and change as everything around me and the business changed, I (the great *I*) doubled down on old ways of doing things.

I needed to bring inspiration back into the business. That's not possible when you have nothing left to give. It was too late for me. I can see these things in hindsight.

Change is the only constant, and being open to change that elevates not just results for results' sake, but that elevates others in the process, will sustain those elevated results. Change for change's sake is not what I'm talking about. But if my story tells you anything, it's this: you either make the changes, or the universe will force you to. The latter means you're playing catch-up or trying to, and in my case, I just couldn't. I was *done*. Being the change agent when you sense there is a better way is far less disruptive and smooths the way forward.

Why am I telling you this? So you can learn what *not to do*. It was a hard way to learn this lesson. I don't want this to be you, your sales team or your business.

The good news is that now it doesn't have to be.

CHAPTER 18

WE NEED A DIFFERENT BREED OF SALESPERSON IN A TIGHT MARKET

WE NEED DEEPER SKILLSETS AND HIGH ACTIVITY LEVELS

Sales and selling must change because in a tight market we simply can't use the same techniques or approaches that worked when the pressure wasn't the same. There is no more room for order takers and glorified customer service operators. **Our companies need and deserve salespeople who can proactively find and create new sales opportunities.** When customers' budgets are tightly held, when decision making is hard for buyers and it's easier to put off making any decision, when the cost of getting it wrong has increased, we need to dig deeper into our sales toolbox.

We need account managers who actively grow the value of their portfolios in these conditions and protect and fortify every account from competitors. Gone are the days of (though I would argue there should never have been) set-and-forget account management – yet I see it *all* the time.

Unfortunately, most salespeople haven't developed the skills we require now. When we think back to the last recession in the 1990s – you know, the one we 'had to have' – we're talking around 30 years! That's a couple of generations in the workforce who have never:

- been a customer
- lived in a household
- been an employee
- been a salesperson
- led a team …

… in equivalent tight economic times.

It's not fair to blame them for not understanding that from now on, sales won't simply come to them – that they must go to the market to find sales opportunities. And while we can't blame them, we must also accept that it's time for us to educate them to succeed in the market we *actually* have, rather than the one we used to have or wish we had.

Around 20 years ago, I encountered lots of salespeople who achieved their targets by working the numbers. They were solely activity focused. Their techniques were awful and transactional, but because they stacked the odds in their favour through the volume of people they met with, they were achieving their targets. So, their leaders left them alone.

These people will also struggle in the current conditions because now we need both: a deeper skillset *as well as* high activity levels to achieve the same results. That said, I only wish I could find these people today! Even though I can't believe I'm saying this, it's because so many salespeople aren't even doing the activity they need to that will give themselves a better chance at hitting targets.

They're not knocking on enough doors, or having enough conversations.

They're not adding enough to their pipelines, and yet they wonder why their pipelines are drying up!

They keep hammering the same opportunities beyond politeness, fooling themselves into thinking that these same opportunities will convert and they'll get their target.

You and I both know they won't.

Bad habits have been walked past by too many sales leaders. We can blame the lockdowns, but I was seeing this behaviour well before lockdowns and well before Covid.

Sales leaders have been content with hitting their targets. Rarely have they asked themselves these questions:

- 'What factors are contributing to us hitting our targets?'
- 'Is there more we could achieve if we did some things better or differently?'
- 'What might my team be leaving on the table?'
- 'Could they have achieved that sale faster or more effectively?'
- 'Have they compromised margin to get revenue?'
- 'What return on time is each team member contributing?'

Activity will matter more now than it has for the last couple of decades. If your salespeople have been able to feed their pipeline with two new opportunities a week, it will now take at least four just to get the same sales numbers because sales cycles and conversion rates are longer and harder.

For a strong partnership to exist between them and their customer, salespeople must now be able to understand how their role makes a difference on some of the key metrics for their company and for that of their customer's. That's when Mutual Mattering™ takes place, and in the delivery of mutual value that benefits both parties there is also mutual enrichment.

How about we start with the upside of the sales team having a deeper understanding of how they can sell in a way that delivers better commercial outcomes for the business? This is a skill or capability I've not seen much in the hundreds of sales-people I've worked with over the last 25 years. In fact, I haven't even seen it in their leaders in any real or meaningful way.

There was a sales leader who exemplified how a lack of commercial acumen plays out. This woman had a habit of saying yes to customers without regard for how it impacted her business. She was an example of a true order taker. One of her larger clients had an office building with five levels, each with their own reception (yes, this was pre-Covid).

Her customer had requested their orders be delivered to each level on different days, which meant cutting up the order into about four separate deliveries.

Her failure to ask the questions a trusted adviser should have failed her business. That large account cost her business money! The large revenue contributed to her target, but that account ran at a loss.

Here is what I would have suggested she ask that customer instead of just doing what the customer asked: 'To help me understand this request a bit more, tell me what makes four different deliveries necessary? What's driving that?'

Now, if the customer had said something like: 'Well, it's not necessary actually. I thought it might make it easier for the receptionists', or, 'I just thought I'd ask' – then the suggested response would be: 'Of course we can do this, but it's important for you to know that for each separate delivery there is an additional delivery charge of $x.

'If it's not necessary to do it this way, I'd recommend saving $x by having us deliver your order once a week to the ground floor reception, and set you up with a regular weekly delivery day. This means one delivery charge.

'Which is preferable for you: four separate deliveries and charges or one?'

Her approach was symbolic of a lot of what I see in the work I do with sales teams. It comes from the 'yes' school of sales which is underpinned by a fear of the customer saying 'no' if we push back or investigate further. What I want our salespeople and our sales leaders to develop is a deeper appreciation of the value they bring, and the company brings to our customers. From that loving position, we actually have a relationship.

Any healthy relationship is two way. Both contribute and it's beneficial for both: I call it Mutual Enrichment™. Maybe that contribution isn't always at the same time, but it is overall. There are more deposits in the emotional bank account than withdrawals.

DEPOSITS

Presence
Time
Honesty
Caring
Consistency
Trust
Doing more
than paid for

WITHDRAWALS

Lateness
Blame
Dishonesty
Excuses
Not following
up/through

Any transaction or value exchange that is one sided means there isn't Mutual Mattering™. Without Mutual Mattering™, there is no opportunity for Mutual Enrichment™. These are the fundamental qualities of those companies embarking on The Sales Revolution enjoy.

A TIGHT MARKET FORCES US TO SHARPEN OUR SKILLS

I am a big fan of challenge because it forces us to stop and think a bit more.

Sales leaders who don't understand cost of sale make decisions that are detrimental to their business like 'adding another salesperson' to the team to hit an increased revenue target.

It doesn't occur to them that instead they could do more with the resources they have or the same with fewer resources. They don't ask themselves enough of the right questions.

There are three fundamentals salespeople and sales leaders need to understand in a down market:

- **How to reduce the cost of sale.**

- **How to reduce the customer acquisition cost.**

- **How to minimise cost to serve.**

Knowledge without the application of that knowledge isn't helpful. I think sales teams need training on how to sell in line with these three principles.

HOW TO REDUCE COST OF SALE

We've explored the costs to the company when senior leaders lack this understanding in chapter 12 because it's not just 'sales' that contributes to this measure.

When leaders and salespeople alike understand the contributors to cost of sale and the way behaviour can improve it, they understand what their contribution to margin is individually and collectively.

Sales leaders should already have their eyes on cost of sale and be keeping that to the targeted percentage. Many only consider sales team salaries as their total cost of sale – when it also includes commissions, travel (petrol, tolls, parking, flights, accommodation), and equipment (cars, repairs and servicing, phones, tablets, laptops). All of these items need to be understood by the sales team, so they also engage in reducing their contribution to this number.

In my humble opinion, even sales leaders who are familiar with cost of sale don't understand the role *they play* in affecting this critical value delivery element – let alone how to communicate it to the executive leadership team or the board! And it is critical if we're serious about changing sales from being a dirty word to sales having a vital seat at the table.

Sales leaders who *are* mindful of this measure and use it as a way to communicate value delivered back to the organisation (which is also a customer) begin to elevate the way their commercial capabilities are perceived.

Their measurable contribution is in black and white.

The company more broadly can see that the sales department is more than a blunt instrument that 'pushes customers to buy our stuff'; they are critical deliverers of financial value.

Challenge forces sales leaders like you to ask yourselves such questions as: 'How else can we achieve this target with the same resources/headcount?' If there is a percentage of revenue that cost of sale must stay within, they might ask themselves: 'What is the revenue lift I'd need everyone to deliver in order to maintain x% cost of sale? Is this possible given: the capability of the current team and the nature of the market? What needs to change in the behaviours of my team to increase their efficiency and minimise cost of sale?'

Different sales behaviours need to become norms now. For example, better scheduling of customer and prospect meetings that maximise time and minimise travel costs, and better planning and execution of conversations to deliver more efficient meetings (fewer meetings to get an outcome with a customer with greater progress and outcomes).

These behaviours won't necessarily come naturally to most salespeople. Education will be required, and new behaviours made into policies and reinforced.

With flights and accommodation costs increasing over the last 12 months, it will matter for salespeople to be able to justify such expenditure when it's proposed. Sales leaders should challenge such requests by asking questions like these:

- If you don't go in person and have an online meeting instead, what would be lost? What could be gained instead?

- Is it a presentation meeting where you're confident of getting a decision to go ahead? What makes you say that?

- Have you tested the solution with the financial decision maker and key stakeholders prior?

- Have you identified possible blockers to this solution? How have you done that? Who are they? What is their level of influence over the financial decision maker and major influencers?

- How many essential decision makers and stakeholders will be in the meeting? How can you ensure they will attend?

- What commitment have you gained from decision makers on the timeframe for going forward post this meeting should it be successful?

- Are there other customer or prospect meetings you can sandwich into that trip to maximise reach and return on time invested?

Where there is uncertainty or a lack of action to find these answers, the travel request needs further examination until there is more evidence that it will generate a measurable return.

It's commercial acumen.

It matters.

Salespeople who understand how much they cost in relation to revenue will also have a different appreciation of how their sales target is generated. They will understand why they can no longer simply ask for a pay increase without also outlining how they will deliver the significant increase in revenue required to pay for that increase.

Salespeople should understand that their cars, their time, their salaries, their laptops and tablets all contribute to cost of sale. Awareness and acceptance first. Then new action (consideration of smarter ways to visit customers in regions, better return on time invested, better care taken of equipment, better engagement when on the road with customers) can be implemented.

It's about dealing with the *truth*. When we deal with the truth (not 'my truth' or 'your truth' but *the* truth using numbers), it's real.

Education creates a different type of awareness.

HOW TO REDUCE CUSTOMER ACQUISITION COST

So, what about customer acquisition cost (CAC)?

Sometimes salespeople have no idea about this measure, let alone how to minimise it. Even their leaders might not measure it or include it in the dashboard to track and monitor. Companies like to aggregate sales and marketing costs over total new customers, which is one way of tracking return on investment and profitability of activities.

What I recommend is monitoring this per salesperson. Why?

Because there will be elements of individual behaviour that will either improve or diminish their effectiveness.

Time or number of meetings will be key here.

As will the costs that go with that, such as travel and equipment, the number of phone calls, lunches and coffees.

You'll be able to see pretty quickly which salespeople have lower customer acquisition costs than others. Those are the salespeople who are generating higher returns than the others for your investment in them. It's important information to have at any time, but especially when you need to demonstrate to the CFO how your team is contributing to the company's viability beyond simply sales and revenue.

Salespeople who are educated about CAC begin to understand why they need to improve their ability to sell. When they see the impact of converting a customer in fewer meetings, in less time ... when they see the impact of being able to see more customers in the time they currently do ... when they see the impact of converting more customers who spend more in less time ... they see that they also make their own lives easier. Selling becomes easier when they improve their skills in such a way that this cost reduces.

To reduce the number of meetings to get a conversion though, salespeople need all the following skills:

- conduct better outcome-driven conversations

- ask questions that uncover better insight and direct customer thinking more effectively

- meet with the right decision makers sooner in the sales process by knowing who they are and planning those conversations

- ensure there is an opportunity to engage with key stakeholders and influencers – often on the same visit

- progress the decision along more proactively

- identify blockers faster

- deliver a solution in a way that will win the deal by clearly solving the priority challenges or achieving the priority goals.

Reducing sales cycles is a fundamental contributor to reducing acquisition costs, and fundamental to this is the ability to plan, which many salespeople don't do well ... if at all! Territory planning, quarterly planning, monthly planning, weekly planning, daily planning, conversation planning.

And what about the awareness of customer acquisition cost for the wider business? What are the benefits?

Think about the summer months when you can smell freshly mown grass.

You step outside after work and the sun is still shining.

There are more daylight hours ahead to do 'non-work things'.

For some of us in the warmer months leading up to Christmas, party season starts.

People start having barbecues and Christmas parties.

Consider a Christmas party one of your suppliers or customers might have.

Imagine you're invited.

Along with you are loads of other people who have also been invited – many of whom may also be prospective customers of yours.

Imagine how powerful it would be for them to hear from one of your customers or suppliers about the value they've received by working with your company. Imagine the picture they're able to build for prospects at this party who may now also be considering your products and services.

The credibility that comes from someone just like them with similar goals and challenges is far greater than coming from you or your company.

Now imagine if one of your employees was also at this Christmas party and was talking about why they love working with your company and giving lots of positive examples of that. Salesperson or not.

The power of a prospect that has been referred to our business is huge. From a cost of acquisition perspective there is a significant saving on marketing for a start because that PR has been done for free by your employee and customer.

The engagement timeframe (sales cycle) is reduced because they have already been 'sold' on you – they now simply need to be 'sold' on how they will work with you.

We reduce the cost of acquisition by having a **Culture of Customer™** in our business.

We reduce the cost of acquisition by having a **Commercial Consciousness™** in our business and when we have **Customer Consciousness™**.

These are at the heart of The Sales Revolution.

They are good business practices.

Customers belong to our business – not just to sales. But commercially competent salespeople are fundamental to success in a down market.

Much of customer retention comes back to customer acquisition cost and the relationship your customer has with your company instead of just with the individual salesperson.

When a good salesperson leaves for any reason it's natural for their customer base to wonder what life will be like without that trusted person they enjoy a good working relationship with. They begin to wonder if it is time to go to market and investigate who else and what else is available.

If a customer only has a strong relationship with that salesperson, our business is vulnerable to losing that customer and the customer acquisition cost is affected because now at least one new customer is needed to replace them.

However, when the relationship is with our *company because Mutual Mattering™ exists* across and through the ways we work together with them in every contact point, through all of our communication and events, how we include them in our business and us in theirs, they may still be sad that one person is leaving but confident about the company's ability to continue to deliver to them as our customer.

They trust us (the company) to provide them with someone just as good – maybe even better – to look after them and help them grow their business.

DIAGRAM: SALESFORCE VS FORCEFIELD™

You see above the four different ways customers are bonded to an organisation. In A, it's to a salesperson. In B it is to sales and, say, customer service. In C, it may be revenue enablement. But in D, that one customer matters and is bonded to and by the entire business. It acts like a Forcefield, protecting them from competitors, and by extending the company's behaviours to become magnetic, customers are held by the company instead of by just one person.

This exemplifies Customer Consciousness™ and a Culture of Customer™.

HOW TO MINIMISE COST TO SERVE

Cost to serve is another key measure that gives a sales leader (and the salesperson) information about areas they may not be aware of that are diminishing the profitability of a customer and the company's profitability. Much of it is determined by the way expectations have been established by the salesperson about what happens when the prospect becomes a customer. Unwinding that is harder than getting it right from the get-go.

When a BDM hands over to an account manager for example, that account manager must be aligned with what was agreed to with the customer by the BDM and then deliver to that.

Like a baton changing hands.

If it is the salesperson responsible for both acquisition and retention or growth of customers in their portfolio, they must think beyond conversion to profitable service delivery.

For an education program to be effective in this regard, salespeople need to be shown:

- how deliveries (if relevant) affect cost to serve: locations, frequency

- how follow-up calls and meetings impact cost to serve

- how value can be added to those calls: new areas of revenue identified, increased average spend, increased frequency of purchase (as long as it doesn't also incur additional costs to the business in processing each purchase), resolution of issues by customer service team in first call, chasing late invoices (cost of accounts people in doing this).

Once a customer comes on board, it's easy for salespeople to think their job is done. Depending on the structure in some companies, it might be – for the most part.

Remember the example I talked about earlier? You know, the sales leader who was acting like an order taker? The one who was addicted to saying yes at any cost? Her selling behaviour greatly increased the cost to serve a customer to the point it was costing the company money to serve and retain that customer!

Examples like this contribute to sales having an image problem. Sales is too often seen as a 'necessary evil' the company unleashes on the market to generate the money required to enable the rest of the company to run.

Selling is one of the few professions remaining where people can earn great incomes without a university education. As such, it's often dismissed as attracting 'less intelligent' people. Certainly, the perception can be of less commercially astute people.

Couple that with many salespeople being relationship-driven instead of outcome or process driven (I know I'm generalising to make my point here) and it's easy to see why other departments in a company can disregard the market insights of the sales team, their feedback and their recommendations.

I'm on a mission to change that by educating our salespeople and the wider business on Commercial Competence so they can communicate their value better, so the business and customers clearly understand the value they bring beyond the obvious.

For salespeople to actively reduce the cost to serve, they need to develop the following skills and abilities:

- how to negotiate an SLA[9] that is possible for the business to deliver without placing overt strain on functional areas responsible for that delivery

- insight into how other aspects of the business operate when they are responsible for service delivery

- when and how to bring stakeholders along on the journey

- negotiation skills.

---

9   Service level agreement.

Cost to serve is one of the aspects of commercial competence and consciousness that can be impacted by and has impact on the wider business.

When other functional areas have not been included in the SLA they may not uphold their part of servicing a customer, and things like the number of complaints may go up. Errors to be fixed may be reported.

Deliveries that are incorrect or go missing or go to an incorrect address affect customers in very real ways and the business too, as these all need to be fixed and redelivered. Customer service calls are made. Multiple departments get involved.

When customers begin to order outside of what was agreed to with no ability by the business to question or validate the reason behind those requests, the cost to serve goes up.

When refunds and discounts are requested by customers in exchange for poor service, cost to serve increases.

Educating everyone in the business about commercial competence makes it easier for them to understand the role each person plays in delivering better commercial outcomes for the business (who is also everyone's customer) and means better service for the customer that pays us money which, in turn, makes it possible for us to have a business in the first place.

Commercial competence goes hand in hand with having a Customer Consciousness™ because it takes an otherwise 'fluffy' concept and turns it into a fact. And when it becomes fact, it's easier to illustrate and understand. It becomes concrete.

CHAPTER 19

EXPANDING COMMERCIAL COMPETENCE ACROSS YOUR BUSINESS

WHEN INTERNAL SERVICE PROVIDERS DROP THE BALL

We've now seen, especially in cost to serve, the impact sales teams can have on the wider business when a contract or deal hasn't been negotiated well. But what if sales has done a great job of setting expectations about the post-sign-up service level and other parts of the business drop the ball with customers? **What is the cost of losing great salespeople because of other areas of the value chain delivering a poor customer experience?**

A customer company of mine imports equipment from their overseas head office manufacturer. This diagram shows how a simple delay to make that piece of equipment can affect the Australian business and diminish the belief the sales team has in what it's selling.

MODEL: IMPACT OF DIMINISHING BELIEF™

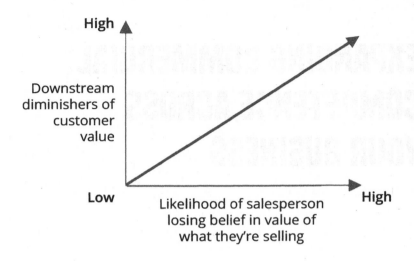

Here's how it plays out:

1   Machinery will take an additional month to be made by the time the part becomes available and production is scheduled.

2   Time to ship the machinery once made is 14 days.

3   Revenue secured by sales in one month but payment from customer isn't received until machinery is delivered – regardless of when invoice was issued.

4   Forecasting becomes less certain.

5   Customer trust diminishes.

6   Customer complaints to customer service and sales increase, leading to time away from other customers and time spent appeasing unhappy customer without any direct ability to effect change.

7   When this becomes habitual (delays to stock availability for whatever reason), customers are more open to more available alternatives.

8   Customers are lost, so annual revenue is lost.

9   Salesperson's belief in company's ability diminishes, which affects new business results.

10   Salesperson leaves because they don't want their professional reputation to be damaged through association with a company that is letting the customer down.

11   Customers leave when the person they trust leaves.

12   Cumulative knowledge, momentum, expertise and experience this salesperson had is now lost to the business

13   Lag period of six months on average before a new person is recruited and productive. And 12 months until similar sales results are produced.

A 2022 study by WorkHuman of more than 2500 full-time employees across the US, UK, Ireland and Canada showed that employees who felt unappreciated were twice as likely to quit.[10] Failing to fix a recurring issue that affects a salesperson's ability to sell with confidence and belief fits into the 'unappreciated' category. Some studies predict that every time a company replaces a salaried employee, it costs an average of six to nine months' salary.

And that is just when one area of the business drops the ball. Who can afford all of this loss in a tight market?

---

10   https://www.unleash.ai/future-of-work/unappreciated-employees-are-2x-more-likely-to-quit/

MODEL: IMPACT OF POOR CUSTOMER EXPERIENCE – DAMAGED GOODS/LOST GOODS™

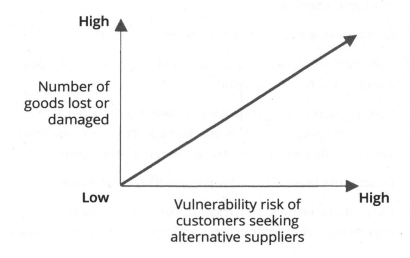

High

Number of goods lost or damaged

Low

Vulnerability risk of customers seeking alternative suppliers

High

MODEL: IMPACT OF POOR CUSTOMER EXPERIENCE – ARDUOUS ACCOUNT SET-UP PROCESS™

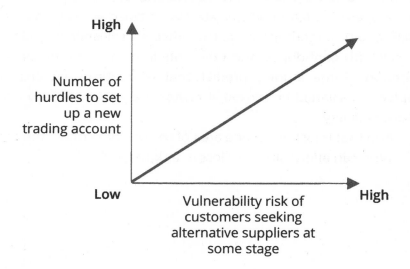

High

Number of hurdles to set up a new trading account

Low

Vulnerability risk of customers seeking alternative suppliers at some stage

High

What role do internal service providers play in delivering measurable value to internal customers? What about the benefit internal service providers can deliver to the company and their internal customers by having Commercial Competence and Customer Consciousness™?

Take for example a customer of mine who has young HR business partners. Now, just because they're young doesn't mean they aren't highly skilled or good at working with the leaders they support.

They are.

What they lack, however, is confidence in their own competence.

And the business has no way of understanding the measure of value they provide to the business and those leaders.

If we give these HR business partners access to the same skills we're developing in our sales team – such as the ability to diagnose the real issue or get to the root cause of the problem being presented rather than 'order take' or just treat the symptom that is evident – they're better equipped to solve problems properly, and save the company money and improve productivity in more ways than one.

In this case one issue was with a leader who had lost one team member and was about to lose another. Besides the damage to this leader's brand internally, it also meant recruiting new people with the associated recruitment costs, lost time and lost productivity as no one is left to do those jobs – and there is no guarantee the same situation won't happen again.

Simply recruiting or keeping the employee who was going to leave by giving her a pay rise for example is only treating the symptom. Instead, by investigating thoroughly to uncover why this leader was churning through team members in the first place, the business was able to prevent it from happening again and saved itself significant time, money and the reputation of the leader, and also developed the capability of the leader which increased productivity in other ways.

But simply solving an issue isn't enough.

What I see in most internal service provision teams is the inability to go back in after the solution has been implemented and conduct what I call the 'value-delivered conversation'. This is where the service provider is able to direct the conversation through carefully crafted questions (yes I know – I'm obsessed) to get to a measure of the value delivered.

The benefits go beyond the actual measure of value uncovered. The appreciation from the business towards the HR team – in this example – would be improved because it would be clear how much money had been saved and what the dollar return on the HR team's time was to the business.

It makes it visible, instead of hidden.

It's actual, not implied.

Along with measurable value communicated comes the confidence the HR business partner gains in really knowing the measure of value they've provided, which is usually unknown as well as unexpected.

In Sales Revolution language, that's when we have Mutual Mattering™.

Mutual Enrichment™.

I reiterate: everyone is a customer and has a customer.

Being of service becomes a way of being in companies that undertake The Sales Revolution. **Everyone being steeped in a Culture of Customer™ strengthens every customer relationship.**

PART IV

MAKING IT STICK

Have you ever said:

> 'I'm going to run a marathon'
>
> 'I'm going on a diet'
>
> 'I'm going back to study'?

I know I have over the years. If you're human, chances are you have too. Maybe you've followed through on these declarations?

Me? Some I have and some I haven't.

I don't know about you, but I tend to make statements like these out loud when I've had enough of my situation … whatever that may be. I finally come to the truth that what has been can now no longer continue – for whatever reason. Actually, it's more than that: I *won't* allow it to continue. I want something different.

Saying I want change is one thing. Taking action to make that change is something else.

But what really sorts the wheat from the chaff is the ability to make that change lasting. That's a toughie. Along the way there'll be opportunities to take the easier, softer road that leads us back.

We'll be tested.

We may even get bored or get sick of the effort.

What I know for sure is that for change to stick, there needs to be more than just a desire for it and being fed up with what is. Making way for a different outcome requires a process of metamorphosis. We can't just do things differently until an outcome is achieved because, what then? If we're not ready to then run with that new reality and continue to the next horizon, we get stuck and revert. It's more than a goal or a destination. It must become our new way of being.

For companies, that requires a shift in culture.

The truth is, when you start to do things differently – when you begin to take action that is effective and consistent – you'll see results show up (usually favourable) that let you know it's working.

It's the same with The Sales Revolution.

Quite soon after you begin, you'll begin to see the following things change:

- increased sales

- improved margin

- lower cost to serve

- increased employee satisfaction rates

- better testimonials

- higher employee retention

- better customer retention/lower churn

- less absenteeism.

Not because The Sales Revolution is magical. As you've seen already, much of it is commonsense and the logical application of behaviours that work.

When we know we're making progress our satisfaction improves. Tony Robbins says, 'Progress = Happiness'. Better results tell us we're making progress. And of course, the reverse is true: when we're working hard but we seem to stay in the same place we burn out: Inertia = Frustration.

In parts II and III we explored the elements of The Sales Revolution, with a heavy emphasis on the contributors to a Culture of Customer™: Customer Consciousness™ and Commercial Competence.

Part IV will show you how to make the changes you've implemented stick so that you can ensure you create a lasting Culture of Customer™. When this happens, you don't just have a person or a team doing things differently – it's the company that is behaving differently. The new culture becomes embedded and behaviours are consistently reinforced and deepened.

That's how you make The Sales Revolution your new and permanent way of being.

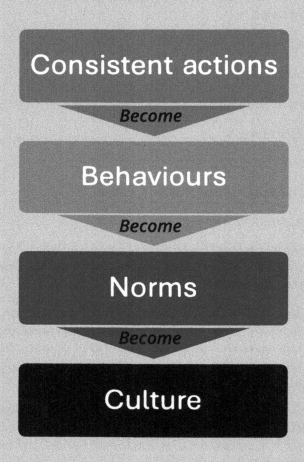

CREATING A CULTURE OF CUSTOMER™

Consistent actions

Become

Behaviours

Become

Norms

Become

Culture

In this part we will explore the six things to avoid so you don't go down the wrong path. We also look at how to measure what you need to change, and I'll give you a way to test the strength of your Forcefield.

CHAPTER 20

SIX WAYS *NOT* TO DO THE SALES REVOLUTION

Some people reading any guide on change will look for the shortcut. I used to do it all the time with the numerous 'self-help' and business books on my shelf! If only I knew which chapter or paragraph held the key, I could save myself all this effort and time reading around it! That's what I used to think. I wanted a silver bullet. What I would come to know is that the journey is essential to being able to keep the outcome. The journey is the remedy – otherwise I just get the relief that comes with the outcome but nothing is really 'fixed'.

The Sales Revolution is a journey, but not necessarily any longer or more difficult than any of the below elements. What it will save you is the large amounts of money, time and heartache that comes from wanting to believe that any of the following aspects will deliver you what will help you *now*.

They won't.

The journey matters because of what we become as individuals, as teams, as companies and as part of our wider ecosystem in the process.

You will become and see all around you stronger people, having better relationships, with improved performance that can be replicated and delivered on purpose, and you'll enjoy sustainable change.

Don't get sucked in with seemingly quicker fixes that may deliver a sugar hit but leave you malnourished. The Sales Revolution may be 'harder' in parts, but I promise it will be worth it.

The choice is always yours to make. Some of us need to learn by first learning what *not* to do. If that's you or your colleagues, I'm sorry to hear that.

To help with this process, here's the What *Not* To Do List.

WHAT NOT TO DO #1: CHASE FAST PROFITS OVER DOING THE DEEP WORK

In a tight market, CEOs everywhere will be pressured to trim costs and increase targets to preserve or achieve profits. It's understandable: without profit, a business is unsustainable and the cost to the people in that business will be significant. No CEO, and no person in that company, wants that.

There is nothing wrong with profit. In fact, it's exactly what The Sales Revolution will deliver. However, when a company seeks the fastest way to achieve profit at all costs or for its own sake instead of changing fundamental business practices first, it will damage its future. When the reverse path is pursued, profits are inevitable.

A fast-profit approach comes at a cost because it usually means cutting costs, and many of those are people costs, which triggers ripple effects across the company that could undermine long-term success.

In 2009, research published by *Harvard Business Review* showed that 250 from 520 businesses in 17 countries whose CEOs focused on cost-cutting were perceived by its people as autocratic and myopic.[11] Employee sentiment was also reduced, and with this came a greater reluctance by them to sacrifice on behalf of the company, which impacted performance. On the other hand, CEOs who put customers' interests and concerns

---

11   https://hbr.org/2009/12/why-profit-shouldnt-be-your-top-goal

first (internal and external customers) were perceived as visionary, generating higher workforce engagement and ultimately being capable of delivering superior financial outcomes.

When in pursuit of fast profits and believing the means justify the ends, it's easy for disasters to occur that impact more than just the people within the organisation. Take some of the well-known corporate disasters like Exxon and Boeing. The fast-profit focus resulted in millions of dollars in compensation, and reputational damage that is perhaps more difficult to measure.

According to a study by Scott J. Reynolds – a professor of business ethics at the University of Washington – published in the *Journal of Applied Psychology*, leaders with a fast-profit approach tended to recognise ethical issues only after harm had been done.[12] The same research also showed that in situations where harm isn't seen to be done, these CEOs seemed much less likely to identify the issue as an ethical one at all.

Boeing's CFO told investors at a recent conference that: 'For years, we prioritised the movement of the airplane through the factory over getting it done right ... '

CEO Dave Calhoun was brought to task by US Congress early in 2024 over allegations of cutting safety corners in manufacturing and maintenance by engineering whistleblowers, stating that maintenance protocols were being eroded by mandate which had impacted customer safety. The cost of pursuing fast revenue and fast profits has been significant:

- In 2018 and 2019, 346 people were killed in two Boeing 737 Max crashes.

- Successive issues have cost the company $32 billion since 2019.

- Customer confidence has been eroded, as has shareholder trust.

---

12   https://www.washington.edu/news/2006/01/09/profit-driven-corporations-can-make-management-blind-to-ethics-study-says/

- Even though he agreed to step down in the face of such heat and potential criminal charges, CEO Dave Calhoun walked away with a payout somewhere in the region of $24 million and $36 million – not a good look for anybody.

- It's only since the recent pressure that the company has committed to improving its methods.[13]

While dead customers is potentially the most extreme example of the impact of chasing fast-profit, any kind of business can inflict massive reputation damage on itself by pursuing this approach.

It can seem reasonable and understandable for a CEO to go on a cost-cutting exercise in a tight market. Without having Customer Consciousness™ they may underestimate the permanent impact those decisions can have on the company's relationship with its customers.

For many companies, savings will be found through reducing headcount. Without understanding the downstream impacts, CEOs who are simply looking at a number forget to see the impact on the customer experience that will inevitably affect revenue and profit which, without insight, could then create a spiral of more and more cost cutting until the company's people are reduced to the minimum required to keep the company running.

Fewer people increases the strain on those remaining. When people are under-resourced and overloaded, quality suffers – whether that's the product or service being delivered or whether it means the ability to provide the level of service required to be meaningful to customers.

When employees sense that headcount is going to be reduced, it in and of itself can produce similar impacts. **Research from *Harvard Business Review* indicates a strong statistical link between a happy**

---

13   https://edition.cnn.com/2024/05/03/business/boeing-losses-outlook/index.html

and engaged workforce and the company's ability to deliver good customer service.[14]

Customers sense it too, even when we think they won't know. According to a 2021 study nearly 61% of customers prefer to buy from a company that treats its employees well.[15] It's only natural that when the people they interact with regularly aren't there anymore, or appear less happy than they once were, or seem fearful or under pressure, it can affect their loyalty and of course affect customer retention rates, which will impact profitability.

Making decisions devoid of consideration of the bigger picture is fraught with major downstream negatives.

WHAT NOT TO DO #2: MAP THE CUSTOMER JOURNEY INSTEAD OF CREATING A CULTURE OF CUSTOMER™

In part II, I outlined the difference between The Sales Revolution and customer centricity, which is the same as mapping the customer journey. In my opinion, customer journey mapping, even if acted on, only changes some behaviours in some sections of the business and usually only superficially. It fails to change the company culture or meaningfully alter behaviours that will drive reductions in cost of sale or improve productivity across the company, nor will it help drive more of the right people to the business: employees and customers.

The experience we give our customers matters now more than ever.

I'm not surprised by the findings of a Salesforce report, which says: '88% of customers say experience is as important as products or services, and 73% expect companies to understand their unique needs and expectations'.[16] But that report focuses

---

14   https://hbr.org/2019/08/the-key-to-happy-customers-happy-employees

15   https://www.fairplaytalks.com/2021/12/22/6-10-consumers-want-to-shop-with-brands-that-treat-staff-well-study-reveals

16   https://www.salesforce.com/au/resources/research-reports/state-of-the-connected-customer

only on the purchase as the experience. You now know that the experience depends on how the company behaves towards all of its customers. And that requires a Culture of Customer™.

This culture drives ongoing performance and a sustainable relationship between the customer and the company. Without a Culture of Customer™, even the most embedded maps will be reduced to a series of 'tasks' to be undertaken by a small number of employees in certain situations with customers. In time, without reinforcement and depth, these too will diminish in consistency and effectiveness of application.

WHAT NOT TO DO #3: TRAIN BEHAVIOURS WITHOUT REINFORCING THEM WITH STRUCTURE

Training people to change behaviours is a massive part of what I've done for most of the 25ish years I've been working with sales teams and leaders. I know that when behaviour changes, so too do results. It's why sales leaders who try to affect sales performance using only a dashboard fail. Dashboards of KPIs mostly comprise lagging indicators that only give leaders a mark of progress to date.

That's all.

Progress markers matter, but we need to know that we're using the right ones. In an ocean of data one easy error to make as a sales leader is to gather all of the available data and pop it all on a dashboard.

I'm challenging that. Just because information is available doesn't mean we use it on a dashboard or to coach performance. **The right KPIs will support you and your teams to truly change the behaviours that will make the biggest difference.** And they should change once the change has occurred.

For behaviour to make a long-term and lasting impact on the numbers that count (remember my top 10 in chapter 3), they must become norms. And for them to become norms there must be accountability, ownership and guard rails.

People revert to their 'set point' – especially when under pressure or when they are left unmanaged. It's human nature. Even the most disciplined of us will stop short of creating pain in the pursuit of improved performance unassisted.

This is why training alone doesn't create lasting improvement. Most sales training workshops are over in a day. While they may have been interactive, once each person leaves the workshop, they return to their teams and the broader business. They may even try to continue with what they learnt, only to revert back because of the existing processes and people they need to work with in a certain way to get the job done. It won't take long before any change from the workshop returns to pre-workshop ways of working. Some performance gets worse.

According to Sales Impact Academy:[17]

- $70 billion is spent on sales training per year in the US

- 84% of sales training is forgotten after three months

- 60% of the companies that do invest in training have no structure.

So, it's not saying sales training doesn't work – it does (it actually gives those who have undertaken training a 57% competitive advantage on competitors[18]), it's that it doesn't last. And that's just one team in an entire company. **If we want to invest in change and training that drives better revenue and profit outcomes, it makes commercial sense to broaden it beyond sales and reinforce it company wide.**

The Sales Revolution creates the behaviours first across the company (Mattering), knowing that without the Forcefield, those behaviours will lack the strength they'd otherwise have. That's why those behaviours are then reinforced with each team setting their own standards, creating routines and structures

---

17   https://www.salesimpact.io/blog/whats-the-data-saying-about-sales-training

18   https://taskdrive.com/sales/sales-statistics

(including dashboards, meetings and KPIs) so that results will continue to improve.

Remember the Growth Model? It needs accountability to be able to have a new awareness, acceptance of what is and isn't working in order to take new actions. Those accountability frameworks may include coaching templates, meeting structures, SOPs, one-on-one conversation agendas, published survey results, company presentations and public performance dashboards. Every team member's value delivery is tracked, measured and reported on. That means every team's delivery of value is visible to everyone in the company – transparency of performance beyond just sales.

Every leader conducts coaching conversations that focus on consistent improvement of how value is delivered and the results that ensue.

If a company only embarked upon the Mattering phase of The Sales Revolution, it would be fondly experienced. Some value would of course be delivered but the longer term positive results may be harder to achieve. It could be relegated to just a 'feel good' experience with shorter term delivery of value instead of creating the permanent change that will continue to deliver better and better commercial outcomes.

You're not going to get a Culture of Customer™ without Commercial Competence. You're not going to deliver value without the supporting structures and inter-functional commitment to change.

That's the truth.

WHAT NOT TO DO #4: TREAT THE SALES REVOLUTION LIKE A FAD

Yes, I'm a speaker. But it's not my primary service offer. I'm not a speaker who also does workshops. I see myself more as a facilitator who can also be a speaker. No offence to speakers in the main but they're often entertainers who are also subject matter experts. There's a difference. Their content is outstanding, their delivery is brilliant. But it's just not enough to change behaviour. It may make us think or start investigating something.

But speakers are not the same as consultants who have been facilitating behavioural change for decades.

I'm not entertainment. I hope to be entertain*ing*, but my focus is always on participants in my programs taking action through knowledge gained, as opposed to knowledge for its own sake.

Those who are feeling the tightening of the market, the impact of more no's than yes's and their sales number diminishing will attend speaking events to see what they can 'take away' from The Sales Revolution. No doubt.

But there is nothing 'faddish' about The Sales Revolution.

It's based on truth that will improve any company's results in a down market as well as skyrocket them in better economic conditions. It improves whole-of-company performance and results – not just those of the sales team. It develops best practice (even if I do say so myself) for all to adopt so all customers love the company and not just those they interact with in the company. *Huge* difference.

WHAT NOT TO DO #5: SEARCH FOR WAYS TO USE AI INSTEAD

AI is here. It's here to stay and it will forever change the nature of work, our experiences as employees and customers, and the quality of those experiences.

Like anything disruptive, some aspects will be outstanding.

Some aspects will destroy.

It's tempting isn't it, especially in a down market, to seek out ways for bots or AI to replace customer-facing or speaking roles? Some companies have already done it. I heard of one financial institution that had already replaced its entire outbound call centre with AI (and that was in 2022).

The consensus however is that bots will be game changing in reducing areas of friction for customers like wait times in customer service, for enabling customers to solve issues in their first call, and in improving the tone of customer communication. What AI can't do yet is conduct conversations that require higher level communication skills such as empathy, compassion, asking the right questions in the right way, responding to nuance, negotiating, and being able to tactically influence.

These higher order skills will become increasingly in demand and require companies to invest in the development of these 'soft' skills for their people in roles where this will be even more highly valued.

Renata Sguario, Managing Director of MaxMe, a company that supports its clients to build EQ, said this of the balance between AI and higher level human skills in my podcast interview with her:

I've been in technology my entire career – 35 years now. MaxMe is a tech company, and our goal is to scale and democratise essential skills through technology. We've integrated AI into our processes, but AI itself isn't a new concept. What's new is how technology is advancing into uncharted territory. At its core, AI automates tasks that used to require manual effort – gathering information, analysing it, and pulling insights together. Now, we're expediting that process, which is exciting for fields like medicine and technology infrastructure.

However, complex problems will always need human involvement because they're difficult to automate. As AI and other automated systems take over routine tasks, humans will focus on what's left: complex work. These problems are hard to solve, where cause and effect are tough to identify, and hypotheses are often the only way forward. To solve them, failure is inevitable, and collaboration is essential – no one person can tackle complex challenges alone. This is where human skills like communication, influence and teamwork become crucial, because those will be the skills we need to succeed in this new landscape.

AI is already saving us considerable time by helping us mine our own CRMs to identify high-priority prospects and customers to meet with, including suggestions about focus based on previous discussions and giving us insights to improve our ability to plan.

That is how I see AI benefitting salespeople the most.

What we must remember though is human beings are wired for connection. Nothing will replace the energy exchange between humans which underpins Mutual Mattering™.

When our spirits are connected, we can feel the third presence of 'us'-ness.

In an increasingly AI world, the people-based experiences will matter more than ever. Not less.

WHAT NOT TO DO #6: GO FOR THE 'QUICK' FIXES

While similar to *what not to do #1*, #6 is about looking across The Sales Revolution and cherry-picking elements to implement instead of seeing it as a holistic solution. The motive is more about the sugar hit than it is about the cost of investment.

In *The Wizard of Oz*, the Scarecrow went on a journey only to discover that he already had a brain. But without the journey, he wouldn't have been challenged to use it or understand its true value. The Sales Revolution doesn't suggest that your company already has a Culture of Customer™ (and you've just got to discover it by going on the journey) but it does suggest you may already have many of the ingredients required to cultivate it. Without implementing it in stages that build on one another, its benefits won't be realised with any depth or longevity.

As in life, there aren't any quick fixes with The Sales Revolution. No one element is a silver bullet. That said, you'll see improvements soon after embarking on the process. Without the program though, they will not be permanent.

The journey will build strength across every team across your entire business. The right people will more likely stay and those who go will be replaced by those magnetised to how you do what you do.

CHAPTER 21

MEASURE WHAT NEEDS TO CHANGE

I work with a client that proudly displays their sales results (both leading and lagging) on television screens in a high-traffic corridor. They're just outside of the Managing Director's office so he can see how his sales team is tracking every moment he glances to his right.

I happen to love visible dashboards. They create a level of accountability that creates a truthful way of taking action. They're hard to argue with: pudding and proof.

But what if every team displayed their performance? What if the company itself was transparent about each key area of value it delivered to its customers? What if each team treated the company as one of its primary customers that mattered and was visible about the way it displayed the measurable value it delivered? **Imagine if leaders celebrated how value was delivered to key customers (internal and external) as achievements at every company gathering.**

Imagine team members from departments across the company being recognised for going above and beyond for their customers or for improving the customer's experience in a measurable way. What if the company shared a customer success story every month that outlined how problems or issues were diagnosed, how the remedy was established, the solution implemented, which outcomes were achieved, and the impact on that situation as a result?

Think about the difference it would make to your company compared to where it is now, and how these ideas could help you to contribute to a Culture of Customer™.

Unfortunately most people see numbers and behaviours separately. We can talk about targets *or* we can talk about the customer experience. We can talk about profit *or* we can talk about culture.

The truth is, we need both. They're both important. One drives the other, and it's an infinite exchange. Without a measure it's hard to manage, and without management, action won't happen. And without action, nothing changes or improves.

When it comes to measurements, I like businesses to focus on three things that create the change they want to see, instead of measuring everything we can simply because we can. The questions I want you to ask to help you to identify the three metrics that will drive improvements are:

- Where are the bottlenecks or friction points in this function?

- Which measures will force the changed behaviour if managed and monitored?

- What is the ultimate measure of success for each team member?

One of my clients manufactures and sells fibreglass swimming pools. Their direct team keeps talking about accepted quotes or contracts out, when these are merely pipeline progression stages; neither of these are sales results. Signed contracts is the 'sale', but this outcome also depends on how quickly they can get an accepted quote into a submitted contract that can then be sent to the customer to sign off on.

When an accepted quote was submitted as a contract, it went to one person to go through with a fine-toothed comb to ensure it was accurate, wouldn't come back to bite them and had covered all bases. Sometimes it needed more information. Sometimes it needed to be reworked, resubmitted and re-evaluated. This all adds time.

And salespeople everywhere know that time kills deals.

Some of these contracts were taking up to 21 days from submission to signing.

So, what three measures did we decide would change behaviour? Just a focus on signed contracts?

- The first measure was the percentage of contracts submitted that didn't require rework. This measure is there to improve the education and attention to detail the sales team put into each contract.

- The second measure was the number of days from contract submission to signed. This measure made sure the bottleneck of one person reviewing contracts changed, as well as ensuring each salesperson took ownership of getting better quality contracts in to start with, and then on driving the process.

- And the third measure was the percentage conversion rate of appointment to signed contract. This measure starts to change the way each salesperson treats each contract from first meeting to signing, with a focus on signing.

Here's an example in that same company of a measure that is ignorant to the broader downstream impact on the company and on cost. It looks good at first but it actually isn't. It's the conversion rate of lead to appointment. When a lead comes in, the service team contacts that lead to qualify it more before setting a time for a salesperson to meet them.

Simply getting them to increase their conversion rate ignores important other factors such as:

- Not all leads are equal: simply getting an appointment – if that's what's going to be deemed as success – says nothing about its quality or the customer's readiness to buy.

- If salespeople simply go to more appointments regardless of their quality, it can make the salesperson look like they're poor salespeople when those appointments don't convert at all or in a timely manner simply because they're not ready. It will also contribute to a higher cost of sale as those appointments still need to be attended.

- The opportunity cost is great. For every low-quality appointment attended, a ready customer can't be seen. That affects sales results, cashflow and profit.

What gets measured gets managed. What gets managed gets done. **Be careful what you're measuring as it could be driving the wrong behaviours.**

Let's take a handful of functions to illustrate my point more concretely.

THREE METRICS THAT CHANGE WHAT MATTERS TO THOSE WHO MATTER

Function	Three metrics of change	Impact on behaviour
Customer service that wants to improve the satisfaction ratings from calls	Percentage of proactive to reactive calls	Heading customer issues off at the pass
	Percentage of call solutions provided that were highly relevant to customer	Increased ability to problem solve and de-escalate issues
	Percentage of calls that gave a separate testimonial to the business of their experience with the operator	Improvement in ability to shift customer sentiment and experience

Function	Three metrics of change	Impact on behaviour
Accounts receivable that wanted to get new customers paying faster	Number of days from contract signed to first paid invoice Percentage of new customers signed in a month trading in the same month Percentage of invoices paid on or before due date	Proactive accounts set-up process Customers included in the account set-up process Link between how we set accounts with customers up impacts the way they pay us, when they pay us and the impact on our cashflow
Human resources business partners to change from order takers to trusted advisers	Percentage of issues with leaders that don't recur Value of costs saved as a direct result of solution Net impact on retention rates per leader	Ensures root cause is established and treated through better issue diagnosis Solutions evaluated more commercially with a view on how costs can be saved as a result of the solution and ongoing costs as the impact of the solution is felt Improvement in team culture per leader as a result of solution

LEADER MEASURES

The Sales Revolution is about collective and individual contribution to customers. It's imperative to have both a collective leadership contribution to customers and that each individual leader is also tracked. The individual measures are for one-on-one discussions with one's own leader, with the exception of the CEO, who reports to the board.

So, what is the approach for leaders to take if they are to identify some metrics that ensure they become models of excellence at creating a Culture of Customer™?

- Identify each customer: who are they, what matters to them, what has been delivered to them, what have they been able to do that they couldn't do before, how has this delivered value to them and to us as a business (Mutual Mattering™)?

- What measures demonstrate a contribution to the Culture of Customer™?

- What customer stories can I share to illustrate value delivery?

Targets are going to be tricky to define until there is a benchmark established. After the first measure, we're able to track progress, monitor improvements or deteriorations, and set targets.
Each leader has a few customers:

- the CEO

- their functional team with direct reports and their direct report's teams

- external customers (end customers or suppliers)

- the leadership team

- the company.

EXAMPLE OF CULTURE OF CUSTOMER™ METRICS FOR A LEADER

Leading	Lagging
Percentage reduction in number of leave days per person	Percentage increase in per-person projects completed before or on time
Net team retention rate	Percentage of total projects completed before or on time
Number of new initiatives implemented	Percentage impact on margin and profit

CHAPTER 22

STRENGTHENING THE FORCEFIELD

A DIAGNOSTIC TOOL

Now that you have established some new routines, some new standards to reinforce and encourage accountability for, and some measures to change behaviours accordingly, it helps to assess those things across the business.

This chapter shares a diagnostic tool you can use to evaluate your progress and identify where the work may still lie. This diagnostic is meant to be conducted every six months, so you can see the progress you've made and celebrate it. And to identify the work that will strengthen the company's ability to improve its Culture of Customer™.

Before you go ahead, I'll explain each section of the diagnostic as it relates to each of the three phases of The Sales Revolution methodology:

1   **Strength of Mattering:** This measures how well the people in the company are embracing new ways of being, how well they understand the concept of 'customer' and their role in delivering value for their own customers, and their understanding of the interconnection between teams, functions and roles in delivering commercial results for the business and a better experience for internal and external customers

2   **Strength of Forcefield:** This measures how consistently and effectively each team is implementing new routines, standards and structures that deliver improved customer outcomes by ensuring awareness, action and accountability.

3   **Strength of Magnetism:** This measures the ingredients that radiate a Culture of Customer™ not just within the company or to the customer that pays us in exchange for goods and services, but to the broader business ecosystem and community.

How to score:

- Rather than simply looking at the total score, there is more value in breaking the tally into the three sections. That way you can more easily evaluate where action needs to be next.

- My recommendation is that you undertake this diagnostic before commencing The Sales Revolution program, so you can establish a benchmark. Then run it every six months until the program is completed.

- You may wish to continue to measure every six months after completing the program, to keep the focus on The Sales Revolution as people grow, people leave (although fewer once The Sales Revolution takes hold), and new horizons are set.

THE SALES REVOLUTION DIAGNOSTIC

Strength of Mattering	Score out of 10 (1 = 10%)
Leaders: Becoming models of revolutionary excellence	
If asked, what percentage of our company could clearly articulate the role they play in directly driving profitable growth?	
What percentage of our executive or senior leadership team is willing to change in order to accelerate profitable growth for the company?	
What percentage of our executive team would agree with this statement: everyone is a customer and has a customer?	
What percentage of our executive team understands that customers are both internal and external and that servicing all those customers to a minimum standard of meeting expectations is critical to driving growth?	
Does each of our leaders understand that they are the model of excellence in delivering value to our customers as demonstrated in their actions, behaviours and measurable value?	
Sales: Ensuring profitable sales growth	
What percentage of our sales team actively demonstrates a commercial approach with customers that maximises margin, minimises cost to serve and drives profitable sales growth?	
What percentage of our sales team is working on the right strategy, right activity, and has the right approach to get the right outcome for both the customer and the business?	
How well does our sales team understand the importance of creating deep commercial relationships with our customers, beyond the transaction?	
What percentage of our sales team is highly engaged and trustworthy across our ecosystem, maximising outcomes for both the organisation and the customer?	
What percentage of our sales team is driven by a desire to contribute and give to every situation as opposed to seeing what they can gain from it?	
Direct: Delivering measurable mutual enrichment across customer-facing and speaking roles	
What percentage of customer-facing and speaking roles are committed to delivering on the value proposition that the customer has bought from a sales team member?	
What percentage of customer-facing and speaking roles demonstrate the skills, attitudes and behaviours that ensure customers know they matter, 100% of the time?	

What percentage of customer-facing and speaking roles actively collaborate across the wider business to deliver a smooth outcome for the business and the customer?	
What percentage of people in these roles can clearly articulate the direct link between their role, the customers they serve and business profitability?	
How confident are you that customer-facing and speaking roles are delivering the same experience (or better) to a customer as the sales team is?	

Indirect: Delivering measurable mutual enrichment across the company-wide value chain

What percentage of indirect customer roles understand their contribution to delivering the value proposition the customer bought from the sales team member?	
What percentage of indirect customer roles demonstrate the skills, attitudes and behaviours that ensure their customers know they matter, 100% of the time?	
What percentage of indirect customer roles actively collaborate across the business to deliver a smooth outcome for the business and their customers?	
What percentage of people in the company see and understand the direct link between their ability to deliver measurable value to their customers and business profitability?	
How confident are you that every person in every team is delivering a Mattering experience to every customer of theirs consistently?	

WHO MATTERS TOTAL

Strength of Forcefield	*Score out of 10 (1 = 10%)*

Standards: Clear expectations of performance for delivering value to customers across the business

What percentage of departments have a set of value delivery standards for internal and/or external customers?	
What percentage of people within those departments knows what those delivery standards are?	
What percentage of people within those departments know how to execute those value delivery standards in their roles?	
What percentage of people across the company effectively and consistently deliver to those standards?	
What percentage of departments measure and report on the delivery of these standards?	

Structures: Systems that strengthen, protect and reinforce the Mutual Mattering™ experience	
What percentage of departments have clarified who its customers are? (internal/external/both)	
What percentage of departments have uncovered what each of those customers value, and what their expectations of delivery of that value is for them in a way that is measured financially, functionally and emotionally?	
What percentage of departments check in quarterly with its customers to conduct the value delivered conversation to elicit a measure of the impact for that quarter, and identify areas to focus on for next quarter?	
What percentage of functional department leaders regularly observe and coach their team members to improve their ability to deliver value to their customers?	
What percentage of functional departments conduct a bi-annual survey with all customers to determine the improvement in measurable value delivered across financial, functional and emotional value?	
Routines: Allow the company to have a definitive reading on progress and achievement of measurable contribution to profitable growth	
What percentage of functions in the company understand their contribution to profitable growth?	
What percentage of people in each function can articulate how their role contributes to profitable growth?	
What percentage of people in the company is clear on the principle of attraction over promotion and its impact on profit?	
What percentage of departments have identified three key performance drivers that lead to results?	
What percentage of functions across the company has visible performance drivers which allow anyone to see progress made in delivering value to their customers and their relationship to profitable growth?	
WHAT MATTERS TOTAL	
Strength of Magnetism	*Score out of 10 (1 = 10%)*
Truths: The habitual actions and behaviours that we undertake in order to become magnetic at a personal, team, company and community level and create a Culture of Customer™	
What percentage of the company's people understand what it means to be magnetic at a personal, team, company and community level?	
What percentage of the company has clear magnetic events (where the business comes together to celebrate wins with and for customers)?	

What percentage of business functions have their truths visible to all in the ecosystem?	
What percentage of functional leaders has set actions against each truth to ensure they're met?	
What percentage of people in the business understand that it's not just **what we do** that matters – it's **how we do** what matters?	
Experience: The measured delivery of magnetism	
What percentage above the industry standard is our customer retention rate?	
What percentage of new revenue is a direct result of referrals from our current and past clients?	
What percentage of new business is a direct result of referrals from our network, the wider business ecosystem and/or from the wider community?	
What percentage of our recruitment comes from our steady flow of talent inquiring about working at our business?	
What percentage of new customers have decided to work with us after hearing about other customer stories regardless of where in the business they heard them?	
Enrichment: ensuring the business is creating a mutually enriching impact for all customers as an inevitable outcome	
What percentage difference does our business make to the lives of everyone who interacts with us (because they're seen as our customers)?	
What percentage positive difference does our company make to the lives of those who interact with us?	
What percentage of the leadership team can articulate the personal impact the company makes to our staff's lives (beyond their paycheque)?	
What percentage of our people is able to easily articulate the impact our company makes to our customers' lives?	
What percentage of our people is able to easily articulate the impact we make to the lives of those in our community?	
HOW IT MATTERS TOTAL	
THE SALES REVOLUTION METHODOLOGY TOTAL	

Who matters:

If 40 or less: There is a high chance that only a small percentage of customers (internal or external) know that they matter to you. The business is therefore likely to be experiencing high loss rates in customers, high customer acquisition costs, low staff retention rates and generally low levels of productivity. There is a high probability people are looking for ways to move out of your company at the first opportunity.

If between 40 and 100: Only one or two functional areas understand who their customers are. I hope one of these is sales! That said, until the whole company understands that everyone is a customer and has a customer they won't be able to connect that to profitable growth, let alone their role in contributing to that measure.

If between 100 and 150: It's possible that there is a readiness for The Sales Revolution as there are green shoots in your company that indicate a desire to do something differently to create a different experience for customers. Some people may already know they have internal customers.

If between 150 and 180: There are more people in your company than less that already have a customer mindset in that they are conscious that they at least are of service to someone they work with, as well as understanding the concept that they have a role to play in the company's success with sales and profit.

If better than 180: There are clear pockets of excellence you can leverage to spread Mattering across your company. Your people have a high degree of customer consciousness already: they probably need to understand what this means for them in their roles and how to contribute to the profitable growth of the business in a measurable manner.

What Matters:

If 30 or less: The level of commercial competence is low or non-existent outside in general. Without this, your company will struggle to deliver measurable value to its customers.

If between 30 and 100: Some parts of the company understand their role in delivering measurable value to customers but these are likely to be either those with external customers or those who work in roles where commercial acumen is required. Lots of work to be done.

If between 100 and 130: While there are some good signs that your people are trying to be accountable and take right action, it's unlikely that the majority understands how to deliver measurable value to each of their customers and the link between that and profitable growth for the business.

If better than 140: Your focus needs to be on consistent and effective delivery of value, accountability across the company in every functional area, and in visible contributions of value by every leader and functional department.

How it Matters:

If 30 or less: The company has a long way to go before it becomes magnetic

If between 30 and 90: The company is growing in its awareness of the commercial and personal value that a Culture of Customer™ has.

If between 90 and 130: The company is beginning to radiate a Culture of Customer™, with more people in the company being able to articulate the impact measures on customers, employees and the company itself.

If better than 140: The company is becoming a magnetic one that attracts the right people to it, keeps the right people in it, and its value is understood by most people in the company, in the wider business ecosystem and even the community. There is a link in most customers minds that a Culture of Customer™ is a loving one that has a felt power.

PART V

MAKING IT MAGNETIC

They say that culture is how people feel about Monday morning on Sunday night. How true!

Before I went out on my own I had a number of roles: one role I particularly loved. The others? Well, let's just say that for some, I didn't want the weekends to end.

It wasn't a recipe for peak performance. And it's not because I was someone who was lacked inspiration or self-discipline. In reality, I had lost my own compass, and with that my sense of purpose. I now know that when my purpose is aligned to the work I do, it's magnetic. There's a pull towards my goals more than a push. That force is greater than me.

I joined the People Team of The Body Shop Australia (L&D or P&C today) – the training department specifically – my first year out of university. After a year of being possibly the world's worst training administrator I was given the most incredible opportunity. Instead of my leader trying to make this square peg fit into that round hole, she gave me a job I had made no bones I wanted. For me, it was the job of a lifetime! It was a national training role for one product group which at the time had considerable kudos. I had licence to create training programs for The Body Shop's makeup range, focusing in on the key contacts in each store who were responsible for training staff and delivering that range's sales targets. Heaven.

I would have done that role on love for that range and the love of training alone. Two of my favourite things in the world combined.

Now, this was before emails and websites: it was the early nineties. So I used all the tools I had at my disposal to drive sales of that category through the roof.

The first thing I did was track sales and publicly report on them using the newsletter each store would get each week in their mail bag (yes: a physical newsletter). Key contacts in each store used to go to my column and look for their results to compare to other stores every week. It was a celebration, but it was also a driver of behaviour: what gets attention gets done.

So I looked at measuring the outcomes that would also mean a change in behaviour. Because it was makeup, I had them focus on makeovers, sales from makeovers and average makeover value. We had a key on the registers to track so we could look at this data. If they were doing makeovers, they were engaging differently with customers: talking about trying on the makeup, using us for events and occasions, giving customers a different experience. A bit more time with the customer meant bigger sales and bigger average spend per customer. Repeat business changed, referral business changed, foot traffic went up and so did category sales. So I took my workshops to stores around Australia and NZ because everyone wanted to be a part of it.

I found it hard to stop doing it because I loved it so much.

I mention this because my love of it was magnetic. Almost overnight everyone wanted to join in and experience the glory of Colourings. They loved it too. Together we loved our customers, and the business changed.

On that theme of love, think about the last time you were newly in love. You may have noticed that you were no longer 'looking' for a partner because you were instead basking in the 'glow' of a new union ... without meaning to, you were giving off different energy: of someone whose cup was full instead of someone on the lookout for the 'one' – or the next one at least.

Because you were now 'all loved up' you became more attractive than when you were looking for love.

People noticed.

Would-be suitors started popping up everywhere.

You might have even begun to think: 'Where were all these people when I was single?!'

Whether it's romantic love or just a love for what it is we do, we radiate a different energy that others seem to gravitate towards. We seem to be magnetic. If I could bottle that 'x factor' I would, but I don't really know what that magic is, and maybe I don't want to know in case it goes from 'magical' into 'scientific' by giving it a logical explanation.

Those people and companies with the 'x factor' seem to have an indefatigable energy: it's like they're plugged into an inexhaustible power source. Because there's no 'neediness', they attract more than they need and have the luxury of discernment.

It's a beautiful thing.

In phase 3 of The Sales Revolution, we get to reinforce our culture – our corporate DNA, if you will – because by now we'll not only be making a marked difference in our financial top and bottom lines, our people will have the confidence to communicate their value to internal *and* external customers. In this final phase, we work on defining the values and qualities that have emerged as a result of our new ways of working and being from each individual, to each team, to the company, and extending into the business ecosystem and into our community.

How we are anywhere is how we are everywhere. It's human nature to be attracted to those who radiate love: those who know exactly who they are and who they're not. Who they're for and who they're not. Who's for them and who isn't. What they're the best at and what they're not so great at. Those who know where their value really lies and carry with them that sense of being valuable and valued.

From that place, we can all truly show up for 'the other'. We can hold space, we can talk from a place of unconditional positive regard, and as such we can tell the truth in a way that upholds mutual dignity.

The Sales Revolution at its essence is all about this type of love. It isn't fluffy: it's good business practice. It's productive, creative and fertile. It's catching. And in business, it's compelling.

CHAPTER 23

COMMIT TO TELLING THE TRUTH

In business we deal with data, facts, outputs, money, technology and people. Even with data there can be a lot of grey. As Mark Twain said, 'Facts are stubborn. Statistics are much more pliable.' Any dataset can be segmented to focus on one element to bring that forward while diminishing another dataset. Without having the complete data, it's easy to see how 'facts' get conflated with 'statistics', and while the highlighted data may be true, it's not necessarily the entire *truth*.

Why am I banging on so much about truth here in a business book?

Because The Sales Revolution is built on the premise of dealing in the truth – especially when it comes to how we do what we do – with every aspect of our being. As I've said before, we can have perspectives, but the truth is the truth: that which is indisputable.

When my son was growing up, well-meaning people gave me parenting advice. One of the best pieces of advice was about truth telling. They told me that if I wanted him to be honest with me, I needed to be the kind of parent my son could tell anything to without fear of being judged.

I mustn't have been able to hear this at first because I came back with: 'But what if he's done something illegal or he's harmed someone: how can I not judge that?'

I mistook judgement for consequences. Judge the behaviour, not the child.

As his parent I could hold both concepts in my head: no judgement of him while also giving him consequences in addition to any that his behaviour induced. By suspending my judgement of him in the moment, he could trust me to hold the space for him to be vulnerable and tell the truth.

Focus on the behaviour not the person.

Personal responsibility for the behaviour.

That can be changed.

It's the same in business.

If we want our teams to have ongoing performance improvement, it's important for them to have the capacity to take full responsibility for *their part* of any outcome or interaction (good, bad or indifferent) instead of wanting to cover their backsides with reasons or excuses. Making excuses creates a lousy customer experience and makes it almost impossible to have anything other than a superficial relationship.

People learn pretty quickly how to survive in a company. Like all of us, they learn through consequences: which behaviours we as leaders walk past and which ones we don't.

Whether expressed or implied, these become the rules of the game of doing business at your company. And these rules dictate how we do things here. This is our way of being.

Central to The Sales Revolution's Culture of Customer™ is the value of truth underpinned by the following six principles:

1   **trust**

2   **awareness: how we are anywhere is how we are everywhere**

3   **accountability**

4   **mutual dignity**

5   **unconditional positive regard**

6   **compassionate conversations.**

I'll walk through each one to illustrate why each matters, how it can be implemented in your company, and what it could look like.

1. TRUST

In many of my programs I've used the Trusted Adviser Equation (developed by Trusted Advisers) as a professional definition of trustworthiness:

> Trustworthiness =
> Reliability + Credibility + Intimacy/Self-Orientation

I recommend checking out this video for a definition of this equation from the developer's mouth:

https://www.youtube.com/watch?v=aISsC9NylUY

What I love most about this definition of professional trust is that it focuses on self-orientation as the diminisher of that trustworthiness.

In The Sales Revolution journey, I talk to participants about committing 'egocide'. As Glen Simpson says about the best advice he gives his CEOs who are members of his Vistage International Group: 'Keep reminding yourself it's not about me ... it's not about me'. When we can truly show up to be there for another human in the way *they* need that to be, we have put our own ego needs aside. It is also known as 'being present'. We know when we are present and so does the person we're with.

But trust building is not just about 'being' trustworthy. As Stephen Covey says, it's a skill like any other that we can learn. It's about what we do, and how we do it. His Trust Matrix (shown below) includes character, which to me again is fundamental to trust: if we don't have a backbone, we'll blow in the direction of the breeze rather than being clear about what we stand for. A company that is clear about who it is, how it is and why it is embodies The Sales Revolution.

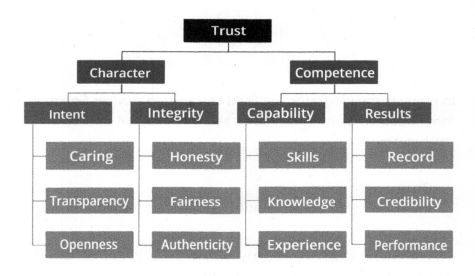

I'm a big fan of this model because intent is equal to integrity. To me, it's not what someone says that matters – it's more what their intent was. Where were they coming from? What does their behaviour actually tell us?

As Glen Simpson says: ' ... organisations have felt that they could put forward a certain philosophy and that they didn't have to actually behave that way. And that can appear to be very successful and very profitable. But it's only a matter of time ... before things break down.'

Words are words. It's the intention behind those words that generates the energy people feel, which is the actual truth. That's how we can hear one thing and experience something else. It's why some things don't ring true no matter how good they may 'sound' or 'read' or 'look'.

We just know.

To get to a set of truths to live by, it helps for a company to be clear about its purpose. Not just tick an ESG box. What that company is *really about*. At its essence – its core ... its DNA – unapologetically and unashamedly.

What would your company be proud to shout from the rooftops that would signal to all those who resonate with that purpose to join? Who would want to belong to that purpose?

How does everything that everyone in the company and business ecosystem radiate this truth? How is this truth communicated? What is the felt experience of that truth by all customers?

When individuals and the company they work for are aligned the momentum is powerful. Like a magnet, purpose pulls people in the direction of what's possible more easily and with less effort. People work in a way that brings them flow: where they lose track of time by being totally in the moment with what it is they're doing and with whom they're doing it.

2. AWARENESS

Anyone who is now or has been a client of mine knows my saying: 'how we are anywhere is how we are everywhere'.

I've heard people say things like:

- 'Oh, I'm only like this at work ... '

- 'I'm only like this because you're observing me, I'm different when I'm on my own with customers ... '

- 'This is how I am on the weekends, I'd never do that in my role.'

We kid ourselves with such comments. We do ourselves a disservice.

Self-awareness is the positive version, the flipside of self-orientation or self-obsession. It is the healthy ability to see ourselves in reality using multiple perspectives and sources rather than relying only on our own perceptions. It is the precursor to acceptance and the precursor for any change or growth.

As leaders, you must build this muscle more rigorously because you're the models of excellence in the Sales Revolution company. **How you behave consistently will speak more loudly than anything you say.** Others will feel 'how you are' before anything else.

Glen Simpson introduced me to a concept called the 'emotional wake' from Susan Scott's *Fierce Conversations*. Emotional wake is the ripple effect leaders leave as a result of their actions, behaviours and decisions that even last long after they have left a company. I think this extends to everyone in an aware company. Asking ourselves, 'What is the emotional wake I am leaving or have left?' is an important self-reflection.

The answers can't be found internally. We must find out from others what our emotional wake is and the impact it is having and has had. Where there is damage or fall out, it's our responsibility to take action to remedy it. That's not just for leaders to do, it's everyone's personal responsibility to own our side of the street. We can't control what others do, but we can 'own' our contribution to any situation: our responses, our reactions. That's each of our jobs regardless of our jobs at the company.

No one is an island.

My programs encourage outcome-driven conversations (see part II) so that every important meeting or discussion has a clear outcome in mind with a structure to achieve it. The format enables us to consider who we're meeting with so it lands for them as effectively as possible. My conversation planners are a tool for better time management, for coaching others and for planning. They're also powerful self-coaching tools because they're one way we can create awareness of what was or wasn't achieved using criteria that keeps our performance in a conversation grounded in reality.

Originally developed as sales tools, the planners have become a tool that anyone can use when they have a conversation that matters. They are role agnostic, so anyone can use them.

To use conversation planning as a coaching tool (for others or with ourselves), I also developed a set of questions to ask *after* the conversation that mattered:

- Did you/I achieve your/my outcome? (yes/no)

If yes:

- How do you/I know? (specific examples of what makes you/me say you/I did)

- What needs to happen now to build on this?

- What new awarenesses do you/I have?

- What will you/I take forward?

If no:

- How do you/I know? (specific examples of what makes you/me say you/I didn't)

- Where did it go wrong?

- What could you/I have done differently?

- What can you/I do to rectify it?

- What have you/I learnt as a result?

- What will you/I take forward to benefit you/me in the next conversation?

3. ACCOUNTABILITY

Awareness and Accountability are both fundamental to my Growth Model. Accountability feeds new Awareness by ensuring we don't live in an echo chamber. It's different to ownership too. Ownership is an internal capability to take responsibility for outcomes and the inputs to those outcomes. Our side of the street, as we've mentioned earlier.

Accountability, however, ensures our humanness is factored into the equation by adding an external reference point. It requires something or someone else for us to be accountable to. Without that, it's too easy to hide.

When skilled, our accountability partner can ask us questions that direct our thinking towards those things we haven't thought of before – into blind spots and dark corners – to illuminate a new realisation about ourselves or the situation. This helps us to gain perspective to balance our own perception.

Accountability helps us to get to the truth and live in the truth of what is, instead of the fantasy about how we'd like it to be or wish it was.

This principle plays out in the following ways in The Sales Revolution:

- **Group accountability:** being accountable to a team or group (meetings and presentations)

- **Upward accountability:** being accountable to a leader (one-on-one conversations)

- **Peer accountability:** being accountable to another team member (accountability buddies)

- **Customer accountability:** being accountable to our customers (value delivered conversations).

4. MUTUAL DIGNITY

In any interaction, my intention is to uphold the other person's dignity and my own. I can't do this without respect for us both. The three keys to enacting mutual dignity are:

- checking my intention

- placing principles above personalities

- asking: Am I withholding truth in any way?

It also means that I am prepared to tell the truth in a way that upholds this principle, which means I first check my intention: is this about me feeling good or is it about being helpful to us both? Will what I say and how I say it move this situation forward?

The phrase I use for this is 'principles over personalities'.

I don't have to like someone on a personal level to uphold their dignity. I can still respect the value they bring, respect their position and their experience. I can respect their humanness without liking their behaviour or its impact.

It's a biggie.

Another question to ask myself when checking my intention is: 'Am I shielding someone from the truth in a way that is disrespectful to their dignity because it's implying they can't handle it?', or, 'Am I about to speak the truth in a way that will cause more damage because I haven't considered the best way to deliver it?'

When my communication skills are well developed, I can be truthful in a way that is clear and kind. It's compassionate – not harsh, and never brutal. It moves a situation forward by framing the truth using this process:

1   When x happens ...

2   I feel / they experience y ...

3   which means z.

4   Check in.

5   Move forward together.

Let's look at an example of how this played out with a customer of mine, in relation to a plan by a Regional Sales Manager for one of his long-time team members. This team member was clearly taking the mickey and using lockdown as his reason for a non-existent pipeline. Despite a few conversations and promises to improve, nothing changed. It was time for decisions to be made in a way that upheld the dignity of both parties and resolved the situation well.

Here is the actual plan (with names changed ☺).

Salesperson

Oliver Jackson

Background

Long history of lack of planning and focus on the key activities and outcomes that need to drive pipeline. Has a poor Q1 & Q2 for 2021. Have already met formally to express my concerns. Second formal meeting to occur on Wednesday this week

Intended result

Determine whether or not Oliver believes it's possible for him to achieve the $600k revenue shortfall for Q1 & Q2 to achieve his period sales targets, each period.

If he does believe it's possible, determine whether or not he's willing to take the necessary action that will enable him to realise this. And if he is, work with him on a clear plan of action that he'll commit to executing as part of a PIP for Oliver to begin this week, measured weekly, fortnightly and monthly

If he doesn't believe it's possible, get him to agree to work with me on an exit plan.

Key message to convey

I want Oliver to decide whether he's in or out.

Key audience

Oliver

Questions to ask to achieve intended results

You're clear Oliver that there's a significant gap in your pipeline that led to our conversation on Monday?

As a result of that, we're heading down the path today of determining where we go from here – does that make sense?

My intention, Oliver, is to support you to take action on the commitment you make today regardless of what it is ... To help me do that, I need to determine whether you believe it's possible for you to achieve the results required for you to keep your place on the team and if you do, that you're also willing to commit to implementing the necessary action that will enable you to achieve those results ... If that's your commitment I'll help you set out an action plan that you can commence as of tomorrow.

But if you feel that this isn't possible for you to achieve for whatever reason, then I can work with you on an exit plan that enables you to start to move toward the next chapter of your life with my full support ... does that make sense?

So, I need to know now which type of support you need from me: action plan or exit plan ... which feels like the right thing for you Oliver?

Exit plan

Okay. Here's what we need to do to make that happen ...

Action plan

Okay. For the first quarter, I need a week-by-week breakdown of exactly who you will meet with in:

- November
- December
- January

Then I'll need a breakdown of the following for each of these:

- Potential value of that opportunity
- Key people
- Strength of relationship
- Intended outcome for first meeting

We'll then set some targets for you to achieve by the end of January:

- Projects
- X meetings with each organisation
- Meeting plans for each of these presented to me at least two days prior to each scheduled meeting
- Scheduled times for infield observation of each of all Tier 1
- Template completed and sent to me each week

So, what is the first action you can take straight away to make this happen?

This conversation was planned carefully to construct an outcome that was favourable regardless of the outcome, and ensured the team member's autonomy was intact when it came to him making a decision. It resulted in this person deciding to exit the business, which was done in a way that was positive for him, for the team and for the company.

We need to get better at having conversations like this, so we're operating in a way that is truthful and keeps us moving forward. By planning how we conduct conversations that matter and by thinking about how our plan will play out, I also ensure I have all my ducks in a row (for example, HR conversations and policies confirmed, support from GM), which means the conversation can be had with confidence.

5. UNCONDITIONAL POSITIVE REGARD

If you're comfortable using the word 'love', then use it ☺. For those of you who get a bit squeamish using love in a workplace context, I have a phrase that is an excellent substitute: *unconditional positive regard*. This is a principle of intention before any interaction. When I show up with love or UPR for my customer, I can put myself aside (commit egocide), hold the space for them, and do it in a way that makes the situation feel safe for that customer. It is one of the gifts leaders especially can bring to any situation to foster a culture that is felt well before it can be defined.

Going back to the introduction to this chapter, I talked about suspending judgement when listening to my son to enable him to tell me the truth. In essence, that's a practice of UPR. It's one of the secret sauce ingredients to a commitment to the truth.

One way to do go into conversations that matter in a 'clean' state is with an exercise called *peripheral vision*.

I like to look out of a window if I can for one minute before any important conversation to do this exercise. As I look out at the horizon, I soften my gaze as I focus on a spot on the horizon in the distance.

Then, I expand my vision on each side (the periphery) gradually to almost 270 degrees. As I do so, I become aware of my environment sensorially: smells, noises, temperature, my body, my breath.

In only one minute I've calmed my nervous system and brought myself into the present moment. From there I am more able to show up with 'an empty basket' for the other to fill with what they want to say. It is the gift of presence – not pun intended. The other person feels this. Because it's so rare, it can change the depth of a relationship in an instant, forever. It takes practise to make this a way of being that is magnetic.

6. COMPASSIONATE CONVERSATIONS

In her book *Radical Candour*, Kim Scott talks about a monk who climbs a mountain and who comes across a fellow mountain climber who has a boulder that has fallen on his chest. The story illustrates the difference between compassion and empathy, and what I'm talking about with the type of conversations The Sales Revolution companies have.

If that monk was to show *empathy,* he would lie down next to the mountain climber telling him how he can imagine how heavy that boulder must be feeling, and that he will lie here beside him as he endures the pain – that he's not alone.

If, however, that monk was to show *compassion,* he would do all he could to first remove the boulder – the source of pain and the reason the climber is unable to move. Once that cause has been attended to, he can tend to the mountain climber to see how he can help him to recover and move forward.

Compassion is empathy with action. It moves us forward by addressing the 'boulder' that is causing pain or preventing progress first, as well as helping the other to recover and then move forward from that place of recovery.

It's genuine and real. It addresses what is, and deals with it in a kind way. Will it hurt getting the boulder off the mountain climber? Probably. The boulder will have damaged him too. Before he continues on his journey, he needs to get better from that damage, and probably understand how it happened to avoid another boulder in the future.

Compassionate conversations are about telling the truth in a way that is kind, and combines many of the other principles we've explored already: mutual dignity, accountability, awareness, and trust. When that is our framework for communication, we are better equipped to *tell **and** to hear* the truth. We're not afraid of it or its repercussions. We are equipped to deal with what comes our way.

CHAPTER 24

THE IMPACT OF CULTURE OF CUSTOMER ON INNOVATION AND PRODUCTIVITY

I talk a lot about being of service, but what does this mean in practice and how does it benefit our business? How does it relate to a Culture of Customer™?

First of all, how do you know you have a Culture of Customer™? Perhaps the truest and simplest test of whether you have established a culture of customer is if you went up to *anyone* in your company and asked them two questions that they could answer clearly and without hesitation:

- 'Who is your customer?'

- 'How does each customer measure the value you deliver?'

When your people can easily answer both questions, you've arrived! It tells you that Customer Consciousness™ *and* Commercial Competence is being practised – it's become a way of being. The intersection between the two is a Culture of Customer™.

But that intersection is just the beginning. Because it's when we build on it further by showing up to be of service to all customers that our company begins to transform into the *felt* Culture of Customer™.

Showing up to be of service is an intentional practice at companies that embody the Sales Revolution. When I practise putting my customer's needs front and centre in a way that makes them feel important and cared about, there is mutual enrichment: both parties benefit greatly. And unlike the sugar hit of 'showing up to get', 'showing up to give' is something that is longer lasting with our satisfaction and levels of joy. So much so that it can become something we seek to do for the feeling it brings *us*!

How does it work?

Most of us studying high school psychology would have been introduced to Maslow's Hierarchy of Needs:

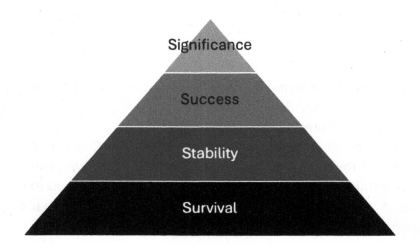

When we show up to 'get', we're trying to accelerate our progression from one stage to another (from survival to success or stability to significance) without understanding that 'giving through service' is how we build something lasting. The truth is, there are no shortcuts because the any gains will be temporary at best. When we progress up the hierarchy by being of service and showing up to give, we consistently build one satisfaction point after another. And these have a massive impact on innovation and productivity. Again: nothing 'fluffy': it's good business practice.

Let's apply being of service to Maslow's Hierarchy of Needs through the lens of a startup business. Some of you reading this will relate to either being in a startup or having started a business from scratch. We've all heard the statistics: nearly half (48%) of all new businesses fail in the first four years.[19] Only 40% of small businesses survive longer than three years, and of those, half aren't even profitable.

While there are several reasons for this, it's easy to approach the first couple of years as being about survival, which can mean trying to do whatever it takes to make as much money as we can. In essence: chase profit first. Or chase profit fast.

We've already seen in chapter 20 why this doesn't work: when shortcuts are taken quality is affected, and even established companies wind up spending more money mopping up the damage they've created.

If this happens to established, enterprise businesses taking a fast-profit approach, imagine what the impact is when start-ups also take this approach?! They may survive, but survival is a long way from success and further still from significance.

APPLYING MASLOW'S HIERARCHY TO A STARTUP BUSINESS

If a startup begins its business life seeking to give and to be of service, if it treats everyone in its ecosystem as a customer that matters, if it seeks to be of value to those customers, it will also benefit because the process of reciprocity has been put into motion. While not the intention, the process of reciprocity commences when someone gives first. The receiver feels obligated to return the favour. It's not always linear – at least my experience of reciprocity has rarely been transactional, which is kind of the point!

Reciprocity may begin by us being of service to our suppliers by introducing them to potential customers. Reciprocity may start by being of service to prospective customers by providing

19   https://insidesmallbusiness.com.au/latest-news/almost-half-of-new-businesses-fail-within-their-first-four-years

them with value that costs me little and delivers benefit to them. While they may not be ready to work with me immediately, they're more likely to want to work with me at some stage, and will certainly share their positive experience with others just like them who might make an enquiry about my services.

Reciprocity with employees may start by giving them confidence in their ability to do the job at hand, or by showing gratitude for their output or progress by thanking them in some way. Showing gratitude reminds me of their value and reminds them that I know they matter.

When people know they matter, they are more motivated to do more, deliver better and value add. But I do it because it makes *me* feel good.

My first business is a case in point. I provided free family daycare for my team, who were mostly mums. I had chosen not to send my own then two-year-old to daycare, preferring for him to be minded by my own mum, and with my mum also providing that service (which I paid her for) to my team, my son had other toddlers to play with. As it was in the 'home office' environment, those mums had peace of mind knowing their child was close by, with no additional pick-ups or drop-offs. That meant I attracted high-quality people, and most of them stayed with me for years: up to eight years in one case, but the average tenure in that business was four years. I'm still proud of that. The entire ecosystem benefited from that desire to be of service to my team.

When an ecosystem begins to grow around the startup, referrals start to come in from suppliers who love working with it because they want other people they care about to benefit from the service it delivers. Growing others' businesses by referring customers to them ends up helping to grow that startup. Positive word of mouth makes emails *ping* and phones *ring* with new opportunities. It takes effort to establish but continues to pay dividends.

In a relatively short while, a startup (hopefully) becomes **stable** with a secure pipeline of opportunities, predictable revenue, stable suppliers and consistent delivery of service. The business ecosystem values the work the startup does, and vice versa.

From **stability** comes growth, with larger revenue opportunities. Because suppliers and employees love working with that startup its cost base stays constant, and the quality of work and output continues to improve. This takes the business from **stability** to **success**.

As a successful business, it's even more able to be of service to others and it begins to expand its ecosystem into the community. It seeks additional ways to be of service to its community through the lens of what that business does. It is a part of that community: the community my team and suppliers and customers come from. It is giving back to that community in a way that is rewarding in and of itself.

Its reputation as a business and business owner has now moved to one of **significance**, where it's known for the service it provides which attracts even more people who want to belong to that business – either as customers or employees – because it resonates with their purpose and values. They want to belong to a company that makes them feel like what they do matters.

Belonging is what happens when a successful company shifts into significance. It becomes magnetic: the right people want to belong to it. Customers, staff and suppliers stay longer and give more of themselves.

Belonging is what our people are craving. Don't just take my word for it though.

According to an article in November 2021, Deloitte's Human Capital Trends report ranked 'belonging' as the top human capital issue that organisations face today.[20] Seventy-three percent responded that fostering a sense of belonging was important to their organisation's success, with 93% agreeing that a sense of belonging drives organisational performance.

---

20   https://www2.deloitte.com/us/en/blog/human-capital-blog/2021/what-is-belonging-in-the-workplace.html

According to this same study, Deloitte says there are three factors that influence a company's ability to activate belonging:

- organisational culture

- leadership behaviours

- personal relationships.

All of these are at the heart of The Sales Revolution methodology.

THE POWER OF STORYTELLING

Storytelling is one of those skills we can cultivate.

Yet, many companies don't actively build a bank of stories it can share with new people who join as suppliers, as customers or as employees. My clients know I refer to a sales asset register, but in The Sales Revolution, it's important that across and through the company we collect and share success stories so that we illustrate how we do what we do with and for our customers (how we are of service) and the value that delivers to them.

When we share these stories, it's more powerful than mere identification, although that alone is significant. According to the NeuroLeadership Institute: 'When we see or hear a story, the neurons in our brain fire in the same patterns as the speaker's, a process known as "neural coupling." ... these processes occur across many different areas of the brain, and can induce a shared contextual model of the situation.'[21]

Add some emotional charge to those stories and certain parts of our brain release excess dopamine, which means we can remember those stories with greater accuracy.[22]

The benefits of storytelling are manifold in companies that embrace The Sales Revolution.

---

21   https://neuroleadership.com/your-brain-at-work/the-neuroscience-of-storytelling
22   https://www.jneurosci.org/content/jneuro/39/40/7920.full.pdf

NEW STARTERS

Trying to get a newbie up and running and productive faster is a challenge for most companies. When your induction program includes emotional stories about your company's founders, about their reasons for starting the company, how the company has overcome its own challenges, how it helps your customers (internal and external) and the measurable difference it's made in the lives of those it serves, it makes sense that these stories are more easily recounted and reshared.

It also means each new person has the ability to speak with confidence about your company to anyone they engage with, in a way that in turn resonates for all of the right reasons. Unfortunately, many companies still only see induction as a necessary item to tick off; that ensures occupational health and safety has been attended to. Instead, it can be a powerful tool that reinforces to anyone new why they wanted to belong to your company in the first place. And we've seen from that Deloitte study the power of belonging on productivity and retention.

CUSTOMER ENGAGEMENT

Customers and prospects want to know that others like them have benefitted from working with you, what that's looked like and what the outcomes are. When they can identify with others, it builds social proof which encourages decision making. Like the rise of influencers on social media, we take the word of others like us (or who we'd like to be like) more highly than someone who has something to gain (like a seller!). Even though social media influencers clearly gain from promoting a product or service, it still works – such is the power of social proof. Told in a story, it's memorable, easier to recall and bonds people together. Magnetic.

CULTURE BUILDERS

In most indigenous cultures, storytelling is central to upholding the shared beliefs and experiences of those who belong to that culture. In Australian Indigenous cultures, there are songlines, dances that tell stories, and paintings that illustrate stories. Every culture has its own set of stories that remind those who identify with that culture what unites them, and what matters most.

Leaders who share stories of challenges and struggles as well as successes and triumphs reconnect with their teams in a way that simply posting results cannot. Stories engage the hearts and minds of listeners, and when done in groups, further bond people together because of the mirroring effect in everyone's brains. We're wired for connection, but belonging is deeper than mere connection. It's bonding. Magnetic.

BELONGING

Recognition of ourselves in the stories of others reminds us why we're here, why we joined and why we stay. We see ourselves in your story. We can see possibility, the next horizon, and what our journey of growth could be. We're reminded of our purpose and values. We know we belong.

CONCLUSION

HARD TO CATCH – IMPOSSIBLE TO REPLICATE

Congratulations!

If you've made it to this point, you may be well on your way to transforming your company with The Sales Revolution. The result of Creating Mattering and Strengthening the Forcefield is to become magnetic. It's where the Culture of Customer™ is present and felt by all who are immersed into it. You know now that when you arrive here, the goal is to deepen that culture, and we've explored some ways and benefits to create belonging and being of service to that Culture of Customer™.

When you're magnetic your company has an incredible competitive advantage that you are able to celebrate and take out into the extended community. From a 'full cup' your company can give back in a meaningful and very real way – even if no one other than that community knows about it – because it goes beyond box ticking.

From this vantage point, you're able to recognise that the community is an extension of your company because your people (internal and external customers) come from that community, and your company is also part of that community.

So, what's the difference between giving from a full cup to your community The Sales Revolution way compared to ESG compliance or as a marketing gimmick?

IT'S NOT ABOUT COMPLIANCE: IT'S ABOUT BEING OF SERVICE

In 2006 ESG criteria was, for the first time, required to be incorporated in the financial evaluations of companies across environmental, social and governance criteria. In my opinion, rather than it being something meaningful for companies, instead it's become a ticket to play. Something necessary instead of something volunteered into.

As you know, I used to work for The Body Shop both in Australia and the UK. When I was there, they were talking about a triple bottom line across financial, environmental and social aspects in the nineties. Not because it had to, but because it was an important component of the way they did business.

They started recycling not because of its environmental aspects but because Anita's first shop in Brighton UK ran out of new bottles and so encouraged customers to bring back their old bottles to be refilled, and eventually, this led to every store offering a recycling drop off for customers to bring used bottles and get a discount off a new product. Its social enterprises came from Anita's family history of having a café in her hometown of Arundel and knowing how important it was for a business to be part of the community it operated in.

This led to paid time for all employees to do community service, and later to sourcing ingredients from Indigenous sources in a desire to find the best ingredients, while supporting these communities. It all came back to smart business that also gave back. At the time it was unlike any other business. But it came from an organic motivation to be of service.

I think it's human to seek external validation before we self-examine, and it can be the same with companies.

Self-examination is where the truth lies, and we must be ruthless in our self-honesty as companies about what we're doing and how we're doing it. Are we trying to *look* good? Or are we trying to *be good* (regardless of whether others will see or how it may even be seen)? Someone once told me soon after I had my son that I'll do my best parenting when no one else is watching. It's true. And it's the same in business.

This is where I think many businesses have lost their north star.

By mandating ESG, the altruism is removed, and for those who see it as a ticket to play, it's an inevitability that they'll 'greenwash', 'gamify' and 'virtue signal' publicly but behave differently in private. Think about some supermarkets that were all very public about the 'YES' campaign for example, but underpaid staff for years and years. That incongruence is caused by a lack of authenticity about purpose. It's one thing to publicly take a stand on one thing yet do terrible things to employees when they don't think anyone will know or it will take years to find out.

It all matters.

If we're not taking care of business, how on earth can we stand on a platform with any credibility on how others ought to live?

One is public, the other is private which eventually became public.

How we are anywhere is how we are everywhere. There is no more hiding. If lockdown gave us anything good, it was the ability to take stock and actually think. We can now smell fakery a mile away far more easily and quickly than five years ago. We've woken up a bit.

I've taken this concept into The Sales Revolution where companies can seek to give back within their wheelhouses – where it makes sense to do so. It's in line with The Body Shop's approach, rather than setting up a social enterprise whose express purpose is to be of service to others by selling products or services to support those programs. I love companies who do this. But it is still different to what I'm talking about with The Sales Revolution.

USING OUR ESSENCE — OUR DNA — TO BE OF SERVICE

I'm talking about a real estate company which supports housing for domestic violence victims. I'm talking about cafés where customers can buy an extra meal for homeless or disadvantaged families. I'm talking about pet food companies that also provide free vet care for homeless pet owners.

What could your company do? If you're an accounting firm, could you give time to educating disadvantaged youth how to manage a household budget? If you're a recruitment firm, could you teach interview and résumé skills to long-term unemployed in your community? If you're a barber, could you give free haircuts once a month to those who haven't had a haircut for a very long time because it's not in their list of survival priorities? If you're in IT services, could you provide a free help desk to an NFP of your choice?

Again, it's not about donations. It's not tick and flick. It's time. It's effort. It's personal involvement. It's showing up to give not get. It's being of service to the community we do business in. Boots on the ground.

IT'S OUTWARD FACING RATHER THAN INWARD LOOKING

ESG to me may have altruistic intentions of encouraging more companies to think laterally about their corporate citizenship. And that's great. But while a company is contemplating how it goes about doing this, much of those efforts are inward looking, with reporting systems to validate the fact they're not 'greenwashing' instead of actually being of service. When we mandate that which would otherwise be organic, something is lost. I'm not poopooing ESG. I'm saying that giving back or just being of service is quite simple.

It requires sacrifice, yes.

And that's the point.

It reminds us that when we have a lot, we have a lot to share.

IT'S ABOUT BEING A GIVING COMMUNITY MEMBER: IT'S NOT A PR EXERCISE

According to Forrester Research at the end of 2022, trust was lost in companies who were discovered to be 'greenwashing'. Now, this happens when ESG is used to announce to the world that 'we're good – look at us'. It's either to shortcut the compliance aspect or to piggyback off the 'goodness' angle with spin. It's not authentic, and customers everywhere will smell that. Gen Z in particular are more interested in belonging to companies that align with their personal purpose and values. They're not interested in virtue signalling. They want to be part of companies as customers and as employees that resonate with what matters to them.

IT'S ABOUT MAKING A REAL AND LASTING POSITIVE IMPACT

A few years back I read about the Dennis Family Homes Foundation and about the Dennis Family Homes founder's motivation of creating communities that were about quality of life for all people.

He was interested in and committed to creating a lasting legacy through his company and its foundation, of enabling more people to live the Australian dream of owning their own home and being part of a community that supported that dream with well-designed surroundings like schools, transport, shops, cafés, parks and recreation facilities. His vision was extraordinary and came from a place different to just wanting to make a profit from building homes. There are many building companies who do this, which again is totally fine. But this company to this day remains committed to this pursuit, which means they enjoy long tenure of employees, suburbs that have emerged from those early building ventures and generations of Australians who have built their wealth from achieving their dream of owning their own homes.

When there is a desire to leave the community better off than when we started because of our involvement, we are set to achieve that. Reaching significance in Maslow's hierarchy and becoming magnetic means we are giving from a full cup.

We give because we have something to give.

We're not seeking to get with a cup that needs filling.

The Sales Revolution is an inside-out job.

It's transformative on an individual and collective scale.

I guarantee you'll never do business the same once you arrive at a Culture of Customer™ and then give back. Never. The feeling is too good.

Becoming unapologetically more of what your company's DNA is truly gives you your uniqueness. **How you are is your differentiator – not a positioning statement on your website or a line your sales team uses in prospect meetings.** It's felt. It's experienced. It's real. When others try to fast track to where you are without going through the hard yards of doing the work to get there, they will pale in comparison. It could be the most worthwhile work you've done and will set you up to succeed for the long haul.

THIS DOESN'T HAVE TO BE THE END!

Just because the book is finished, doesn't mean that's it! Taking action is the key to change and there are lots of ways to work with Ingrid so you don't go back to 'old' ways of working.

GET IN TOUCH

Start a conversation with Ingrid:

LinkedIn: linkedin.com/in/IngridMaynard/
Email: ingrid@thesalesdr.com.au
Website: www.thesalesdr.com.au/contact/

BOOK INGRID FOR YOUR SALES CONFERENCE, EXECUTIVE OFF SITE OR EVENT

Ingrid's 25-year track record of transforming business outcomes in record time frames for some of Australia and New Zealand's most iconic brands means you know she is speaking from experience – not theory, so you're in a credible pair of hands!

She has featured on Sky Business, Ticker News, as a regular contributor to CEO World, the *Daily Telegraph* and *Herald Sun*. You want your people to tell you how Ingrid's keynote made them feel re-energised and inspired to take action! Imagine a room of your people laughing, sharing ideas to action and a newfound sense of purpose?

Bring focus to your next event with keynote workshop topics such as:

1. **It's time for the Sales Revolution**
2. **How to create a Culture of Customer**
3. **No more order takers and glorified customer service agents!**
4. **The hidden opportunities in a tight market**
5. **Make your company a profit magnet**

BESPOKE TRAINING, CONSULTING AND COACHING FOR YOUR COMPANY

The Sales Doctor is seen as the 'go-to' for corporations who want a bespoke approach to their unique set of challenges. You'll walk the journey together. Getting better outcomes means change. Ingrid speaks what must be acknowledged and actioned with compassion. Maybe it's the secret sauce that elevates her client's perceptions of what's possible for themselves and for their organisations? Find out for yourself.

Proof lies in the results:
- **$2m sales in a month being a celebration to being the norm; now, $3.5m is the benchmark**
- **20% conversion rates on pitches to 80%**
- **$500m target reached in 4 years instead of 5**

ENROL IN THE SALES DOCTOR SCHOOL

Online programs target salespeople, consultants and leaders from beginners to experienced professionals looking for ways to get an edge.

For focused, low-touch, self-paced learning for individuals and teams contact us at:

grow@thesalesdr.com.au

LISTEN TO THE SALES REVOLUTION PODCAST

Join The Sales Revolution Community by **following the podcast** on Spotify.